SKI

FIFTY YEARS IN

N O R T H   A M E R I C A

BY RICHARD NEEDHAM

HARRY N. ABRAMS, INC., PUBLISHERS, NEW YORK

Editor: Robert Morton
Assistant Editor: Harriet Whelchel
Designer: Bob McKee
Photo Editor: John Crowley

Library of Congress Cataloging-in-Publication Data
Needham, Richard.
  Ski: fifty years in North America.
    1. Skis and skiing—United States—History.
2. Skis and skiing—Canada—History.
I. Title.
GV854.4.N42   1987
796.93'0973   87–1114
ISBN 0–8109–1504–9

Published in 1987 by Harry N. Abrams,
Incorporated, New York
Times Mirror Books
Printed and bound in Japan

C O N T E N T S

INTRODUCTION

First, this is not a book of records. You want records? Read the record books.... You want serious? You won't find that here, either. Is skiing, after all, an occasion for seriousness?

This is a book about people, about passion, about a nation's fifty-year love affair with a sport so personal, so pleasurable, so entirely all-consuming that to treat it as an exercise in numbers, dates, and historical bric-a-brac would be like describing Chopin's Polonaise no. 6 by its number of sixteenth notes.

I have a confession to make. Although I've been editing SKI Magazine for more years than I care to count, I've learned more about the sport in the twelve months it has taken to compile the remembrances in these pages than I have in the last twenty years. I am still, I can say unabashedly and without blushing, a student of the sport. And that's fine with me since, like skiing, the real fun in history poking is in discovery, in the learning.

Whenever you announce that you are "doing" a ski book, you can be sure there will be plenty of people around offering to help you do it right. Just as everything we learn in skiing is learned from those who went before, I owe most of what you will read and see in these pages to those who went before—the visionaries responsible for bringing the resorts, the techniques, the gadgets, the sheer fun of skiing so vividly and penetratingly to our lives. And these include the observers,

the writers, editors, and reporters whose work has for fifty years so colorfully graced the pages of SKI Magazine: Morten Lund, John Fry, I. William Berry, Peter Miller, Abby Rand, Martie Sterling, and others.

There have been other storytellers, consummate weavers of romantic, sometimes ribald, yarns whose love for America's favorite winter pastime shines through in such works as *Ski Down the Years* (John Jay), *SKI Magazine's Encyclopedia of Skiing* (Robert Scharff), *The Great North American Ski Book* (I. William Berry), *Sun Valley:* (Dorice Taylor), *America's Ski Book* (the editors of SKI Magazine), and *A Pictorial History of Downhill Skiing* (Stan Cohen). For these important contributions to the literature of the sport, and to their authors, I am indebted.

I—we—owe much to these folks. Without them, you and I at this moment would probably be snuggled up with another book—say *The Adventures of Sherlock Holmes*. But then even Holmes's creator, Sir Arthur Conan Doyle, had skiing on his mind. In 1894 he wrote:

> *There is nothing peculiarly malignant in the appearance of a pair of "ski." No one to look at them would guess at the possibilities which lurk in them. But you put them on, and you turn with a smile to see whether your friends are looking at you, and then the next moment you are boring your head madly into a snowbank, and kicking frantically with your feet . . . and your friends are getting more entertainment than they had ever thought you capable of giving.*

With photographs by
Peter Arnold,
Bruce Barthel,
Margaret Durrance,
Mike Epstein,
James Kay,
Jerry LeBlond,
David Madison,
Fletcher Manley,
and others

PART I
THE BEGINNING

Previous page: *Coeds on a ski spree. In the twenties ski apparel had not yet come out of the closet.*

Depression and unemployment were rampant. Elections in Spain touched off a civil war. Shirley Temple was *the* child star. The Duchess of Kent introduced eye veils on hats. Hitler invaded the Rhineland. George V died and brought black into fashion. Art Deco was "in." American farming, plagued by overproduction and low prices, hit the skids. Edward VIII abdicated the British throne. American sprinter Jesse Owens captured four Olympic gold medals. Marlene Dietrich enchanted American filmgoers. Margaret Mitchell wrote *Gone with the Wind.* W. H. Auden, Stephen Spender, and George Orwell became Communists.

The 1930s were a mixed bag. Hopeful, bleak, fear ridden, chaotic, they were also in the United States the milieu against which the modern era of skiing, an antidote to the tumultuous times, developed. "The great game," SKI Magazine's Morten Lund later reported, "was to forget world politics and the economy and concentrate on whether or not you could make a no-fall run."

If skiing wasn't entirely new to Americans in 1936—the nation's first ski school had been established in 1929 in New Hampshire and rope tows were already carrying skiers to U.S. mountaintops—it also certainly wasn't very popular either.

A series of events changed all that.

In 1936 the nation's first "destination" ski resort—a winter playground requiring a significant commitment in time and money to reach—opened. Sun Valley was the brainchild of William Averell Harriman, the young, dashing, polo-playing president of the Union Pacific Railroad. Harriman, anxious to increase Union Pacific passenger traffic to the West, knew he needed a destination that would attract new business. The question was, where? He had met young Austrian noble-man-mountaineer Count Felix Schaffgotsch, who had been sent by his family to New York to learn American banking methods. Harriman took an immediate liking to the adventuresome count, put him on the payroll, and pointed him west with instructions to find the "perfect location for a winter resort." Harriman's one condition was that the place be reached by the Union Pacific line. After months of slogging the deep snows of Mount Rainier, Mount Hood, Yosemite, Lake Tahoe, Utah, Colorado, and Jackson Hole, Wyoming, a discouraged Count Felix headed for Denver for his return east and to report to Harriman that he had failed to find a location for the perfect winter resort. But just before boarding the train, he was called by Bill Hynes, the Union Pacific freight agent who had squired the count and his six pairs of skis around the West. Hynes, who had parted company with the count in Pocatello, had trained to Boise where a coworker suggested to him that the count should have a look at Ketchum, a mining-day relic and Union Pacific outpost that had taken more money to keep its branch line open in winter than any other branch on the railroad. Hynes wired the count in Denver and the count caught the first train to Ketchum—at the time, in the words of longtime Sun Valley publicist Dorice Taylor, "little more than a wide spot in a road that led to nowhere." After three days of skiing Ketchum's snowy foothills, each one a perfect ski slope rolling up from a windless valley, the count had discovered what he was looking for: sun, powder snow, treeless Alpine terrain, a valley sheltered from the northern wind, and a remoteness that would leave the place accessible in winter only to passengers of the Union Pacific Railroad. Wrote the count to Harriman, "Among the many attractive spots I have visited, this combines more delightful features than any place I have seen in the United States, Switzerland, or Austria for a winter sports resort."

In 1936 construction on the Sun Valley Lodge began and Harriman hired Steve Hannagan, the flamboyant publicity genius who had put Miami Beach on the map, to bring the world to Ketchum. It was not a marriage made in heaven. Hannagan hated snow and didn't believe that anyone in his right mind would put on a pair of skis. Dorice Taylor, in her book *Sun Valley:*, described Hannagan's reaction: "We looked around and all I could see was just a godforsaken field of snow. All I had on was a light tweed suit...and it was colder than hell. 'This is strictly ridiculous,' I said, but we walked around some more with my shoes full of snow, and then the sun came out. Soon I opened my coat. Pretty soon I took it off and opened my vest. Then I began to sweat. You know, the temperature goes up to ninety-seven there in the sun and still the snow doesn't melt."

The opening of the Sun Valley Lodge, replete with Hollywood stars and starlets whose presence Hannagan had assured, was anything but auspicious. For one thing, it failed to snow, leaving guests little to do but eat and drink. For another, David Selznick had put his fist squarely into the face of another guest who, in a tipsy state, had asked actress Joan Bennett, who was sitting at Selznick's table, to dance. Hannagan, apprised in New York by long distance of this embarrassing turn of events, could hardly contain his excitement. "What do you mean the party's ruined?" he shouted. He then sat down at his typewriter to prepare his release, and wrote the headline, SUN VALLEY OPENS WITH A BANG.

In its early years Sun Valley attracted the stars—Tyrone Power, Ingrid Bergman, Gary Cooper, Clark Gable, Margaret Sullavan, Norma Shearer, Merle Oberon, Van Johnson, Rosalind Russell, Myrna Loy, Loretta Young, Jimmy Stewart, and Ernest Hemingway (who later settled in Sun Valley).

It also brought others, among them the notorious Virginia Hill, former paramour of late Chicago gangster Bugsy Siegel. The Siegel mob thought a remote sanctuary like Sun Valley just dandy for someone with Miss Hill's loose tongue. So there she was deposited, provisioned once a month by a limousine whose occupants would drop off shoe boxes full of cash to keep Miss Hill content, and quiet, in her new environment. Her story, however, was not a happy one. Virginia Hill fell in love with Sun Valley ski instructor Hans Hauser, married the dashing Austrian, fled with him to Europe, had a son, and, when the shoe boxes of cash no longer arrived from America, committed suicide.

With its outdoor swimming pool, private cottages, elegant dining, continual entertainment, and a clientele studded

Opposite, above: *Midwinter carnival chorines at the Knox School in Cooperstown, New York. Ski clothing, before stretch pants, still had an eclectic touch.*

Opposite, below: *Bunny Bertram's rope tow in Woodstock, Vermont, America's first, was as much a drawing card as the hill itself.*

Left: *The Marquis d'Albizzi performs a flawless Christiania in front of the Lake Placid Lodge.*

with society names and movie stars, Sun Valley easily would have made it as "America's first winter resort." But its importance for skiing went beyond that. It was also home of the world's first chair lift, designed in 1936 by Union Pacific engineer Jim Curran, who had once helped build equipment for loading bananas in the tropics. Curran experimented with the chair-lift idea at the Union Pacific's railroad shops in Omaha, Nebraska. Needing to know the speed at which the moving chair could safely scoop up skiers, he built a boom on the back of a pickup truck, suspended a chair from it, then drove alongside a test skier, experimenting to find the right speed. That determined, hooks that handled bananas were replaced by chairs, and the Sun Valley chair lift was born—to change the sport forever.

If Sun Valley was to revolutionize the idea of winter vacationing, the 1936 Olympic Winter Games at Garmisch-Partenkirchen, Germany, would bring skiing to even greater public attention. The Garmisch Games were the first to recognize Alpine skiing as an Olympic event; previously, cross-country and ski jumping were the only events. The 1936 Winter Olympics also marked the debut of America's first Alpine Olympic ski team. America's top racer of the era was Dartmouth's Dick Durrance, who, having seen snow only for the first time at the age of thirteen, had captured the German national junior title while an elementary school student in Garmisch. (Durrance's mother, an educator, was adamant about schooling her children in Germany.) Durrance took eighth in the slalom in his thrashing, daredevil style, and eleventh in the downhill—which, due to the flatness of the course, was run at a tortuously slow average speed of 26 miles per hour. Austria's Anton "Toni" Seelos, selected as a slalom forerunner because he had been barred from Olympic competition as a professional—he had taught skiing at Saint Anton—beat the winning time by five seconds.

With these developments, and more on the horizon, the time was ripe for a national ski publication, a source of news and views on the sport that would keep North America's thirsty ski public informed. Enter SKI Magazine in 1936. Seattle newspaperman Alf Nydin, SKI's editor, promised in the magazine's maiden issue to "entertain and enlighten...with humor, fashions, and photographs of mountain splendors."

There was much to report on in the 1930s. Although ski lifts, to stretch the term, had been around for some time (in the 1880s schoolboys in Johnsonville, California, with skis in hand, rode ore-bucket conveyor belts up to the Plumas-Eureka mine), the first uphill conveyance to gain serious skier attention was the rope tow. Also called "Up Ski," a somewhat more "in" term at the time, the rope tow was invented in 1932 by Alex (nickel a ride) Foster at Shawbridge, Quebec. It soon became overshadowed by more exotic uphill conveyances, such as the J-bar, which first appeared in 1935 near the campus of Dartmouth College at Hanover, New Hampshire; the chair lift (Sun Valley, 1936); the aerial tramway (Cannon Mountain, New Hampshire, 1938); and the T-bar (Pico Peak, Vermont, 1940). No matter. The much-maligned rope tow,

Opposite: *Averell Harriman in 1953,
basking in what Sun Valley is famous for
with the racer that the Idaho resort is
famous for: Gretchen Fraser, winner of
America's first Olympic medals—gold
and silver—in 1948.*

which would go on to provide the bulk of uphill transportation for the next twenty years, was idolized and romanticized by legions of American practitioners of the sport. If nothing else, a skier's rope-tow adventures were always good conversation openers.

Riding this country's first rope tow, at Suicide Six in Woodstock, Vermont, became something of a sport in itself. As one local newspaper headlined the story in 1941, "Bunny Bertram Provides New Thrills with New 100MPH Tow for Skiers Finding Suicide Six Too Easy." Bertram—who was a he not a she—was the owner and operator of the rope tow at Suicide Six. Wendy Morse—also a he—set an uphill speed record of 91 miles per hour on Bertram's rope tow. It wasn't until six years later, in 1947, that Italian racer Zeno Colo set a new *downhill* speed record of 99 miles per hour.

Such sporting feats notwithstanding, most skiers of the time were happy to see other forms of uphill transportation evolve. As SKI reported, "Most people think the important thing about skiing is getting down the slope without losing an arm. They're wrong. The important thing is getting *up* the slope without losing an arm. The guy who invented the rope tow should have been towed up a tree with a rope, and we don't mean under his armpits."

The rope tow attracted throngs of skiers from Maine to Washington. And thousands of them came by the ubiquitous snow trains—the "Skimeisters" and "Snow Clippers"—that clacked and chugged their way into the mountains of New England, Michigan, Washington, Colorado, and California. There they met the bronzed, godlike, German-accented ski instructors: Sig Buchmayr, director of America's first ski school at Peckett's-on-Sugar Hill in New Hampshire; Hans Hauser and Otto Lang of Sun Valley; Luggi Foeger at Yosemite, California; Otto Schniebs ("Skiing is not shust shport—it is a vay uf life!") at Dartmouth; Stowe's Sepp Ruschp; and . . . Hannes Schneider.

Hannes Schneider didn't exactly invent Alpine skiing, but most who came under his influence would probably tell you otherwise. Schneider, a shaggy-haired, owl-faced ski instructor from Saint Anton, Austria, was apprenticed by his father to become a cheesemaker. But Hannes had other things in mind. He loved to ski, and he loved to teach others to ski. He had, as a result, cultivated an eager clientele at Saint Anton based on a teaching approach that was easy and fun to learn. Schneider had vision, an uncanny analytical ability, a sense of the dramatic, and, above all, the ability to put himself in the skier's, particularly the beginner's, boots.

Prior to the 1930s few Americans had mastered the formal techniques of Alpine skiing, most having learned whatever they could from friends. Back in Europe, after seeing combat in World War I, Schneider returned to the Arlberg and the goal of making skiing fun and easy to learn. He trained instructors such as Luggi Foeger, Otto Lang, Benno Rybizka, Friedl Pfeifer, and Sepp Ruschp, all of whom were uneasy with what Hitler was doing next door and who began thinking, like

Below: *Count Felix looks on as instructor Hans Hauser prepares his ski bases in the wax room of the Sun Valley Lodge.*

Opposite, above: *Experiments with the moving chair lift made by Union Pacific engineer Jim Curran at the Union Pacific shops in Omaha, Nebraska, were enthusiastically endorsed by Averell Harriman.*

Opposite, below: *Curran's marvelous "people scooper" in operation at Sun Valley*

many Austrians, about living elsewhere. These, and others, emigrated to the United States to become legends during the sport's formative years.

Schneider drilled his instructors with a discipline that made them unique in the world. "Control first, speed will come later" was the essence of Schneider's teaching approach. Pupils learned the snowplow turn, then the stem turn, progressively reducing the stem until the skis were almost parallel throughout the turn. Finally, Schneider organized the various maneuvers into a logical system in which the pupil learned one maneuver, then another one more advanced. The drop-knee telemark turn, historically the accepted method of maneuvering a pair of skis, fell quickly into disfavor.

"The key to Schneider's approach," wrote SKI's John Fry, "was his technique, which was accomplished by a shifting of the skier's weight and upper-body rotation. Disciples of Schneider were often more doctrinaire than Schneider himself in interpreting his technique, with the result, in tradition-bound schools, that some pupils seldom got beyond the stem position. It was ironic, since Schneider himself skied with little affectation, was against rigidity in ski teaching, and wanted to get his pupils to the stage of parallel skiing faster."

Hitler's rise brought about the decline of tourism and skiing in the Arlberg, and, following the Anschluss in 1938, Schneider was jailed by the Nazis. Through the efforts of Harvey Gibson, then the head of a New York bank and the financial backer of the United States' first tracked lift—the cog-operated Skimobile at Mount Cranmore, New Hampshire—Schneider's transit to America was arranged in 1939.

"Hannes Schneider's arrival in North Conway," wrote Fry, "befitted the coming of the Messiah. Church bells rang, a band played, and 150 young skiers made an archway of raised ski poles for Schneider's triumphal appearance."

With Schneider's arrival, America went Alpine-crazy. Some, consumed by their enthusiasm, began taking potshots at "those Nordic types." "We cannot but feel," reported the *Mount Mansfield Bulletin* in 1940, "that the proponents of cross-country skiing are wasting their time trying to popularize it. Some things just have not got what it takes to be universally popular, and ski touring is one of them. Touring requires imagination and an appreciation of solitude, which the majority of people do not have and do not want."

Schneider, who immediately set about creating America's first groomed ski run by cutting down trees and clearing the south slope of Mount Cranmore, was amazed at how eagerly Americans took to the sport, finding them much more serious about learning than Europeans of the time.

At the same time, he was concerned that American skiers might be too anxious, impulsive in their quest for speed without first having learned the finer points of the sport. Cautioned Schneider, "It is better, safer, and sportier to ski with absolute control than to schuss down with only a prayer on your lips."

Impressed though he was with the Americans' spirit, Schneider did not think much of the American skier's equipment, which he blasted as "shoddy... boots which I can almost fold up and put into my pocket, bindings which do not fit, skis of the most peculiar type and construction. A lot of tin-and-cardboard is what we would call it in Austria."

Opposite: *The Sun Valley Lodge, and Dollar Mountain beyond, seen from Dollar Mountain Road. Buses still shuttle between Dollar and Bald mountains today.*

Below: *Hannes Schneider was an inspiration to all skiers, young or old. Here he helps a youngster get his gear together for an Arlberg lesson at Mount Cranmore, New Hampshire.*

Most would agree with Schneider that the type of equipment that characterized the skier of the thirties was peculiar, requiring all manner of bodily contortions in order to turn and control it. Leather boots were soft, cable bindings were loose and inefficient, and skis—now *there* was something you could really talk about. And one ski that skiers of the day talked most about was the Eriksen.

The Eriksen, introduced in 1935, was the work of Norwegian ski makers Bjorn Ullevoldsaeter and Marius Eriksen, the latter a man who had invented the original "beartrap" toe iron and the partial edge used on the Eriksen ski. He also sired a son named Stein.

Though the solid-wood Eriksen ski differed little in construction from earlier types, it was the most responsive ski of its time. Wooden skis with a turned up tip dated back some forty-five-hundred years. But earlier skis were dimensionally uniform throughout their length—and the Eriksen had a real shape to it. Its wide forebody, soft tip, and soft tail allowed the skier to initiate a turn quickly, then bend the ski into an arc, causing the ski to carve, rather than skid, through the snow. Adding to its turning ability was the Eriksen's "ridge top," which allowed the ski to bend into an even more pronounced arc without breaking.

The Eriksen's greatest fan, the man who *was* the United States Ski Team in 1936, was Dick Durrance, who rode his Eriksens to a combined tenth-place finish at the 1936 Winter Olympics. "Durrance's success on the Eriksen," Morten

Lund wrote later, "gave competitive skiing an image that American college kids could identify with—something dashing and sexy, like wing walking."

As the thirties advanced, so too did ski design, and the array of choices—flat tops, dome tops, laminates, semiflat tops, ridge tops—suddenly became all too confusing. One thing most skiers agreed upon, however: laminate skis worked best. This construction—also developed by Bjorn Ullevoldsaeter—led to a stronger, more resilient ski than was possible with solid hickory construction. Thin layers of wood were glued together, much like plywood, in narrow strips called "cane" throughout the length of the ski. Thus the ski was of a "split cane" (*splitkein* in Norwegian) construction. Licensing rights to produce Splitkein skis in the United States were obtained by Thor Groswold, a Norwegian who had emigrated to Denver, and by the Northland ski factory in Saint Paul, Minnesota. To own a laminate ski in the thirties was to set yourself apart, and the more laminations your ski possessed the more expert a skier you were considered to be.

If Americans were scratching their heads over the proliferation in ski design, the proper technique for turning a pair of skis was no less confusing. At about the same time that the Arlberg technique was being preached according to the gospel of Hannes Schneider, a Frenchman by the name of Emile Allais was experimenting with another method. Allais, who had won the 1937 Alpine World Championships, sanctioned by the Fédération Internationale de Ski (FIS), had written a book that showed yet another, more efficient way to turn a pair of skis. It was called parallel skiing and it was adapted by Allais from a technique pioneered by Austrian ski instructor Toni Seelos. Seelos's technique was characterized by upward unweighting, upper-body rotation, as in Hannes Schneider's Arlberg technique, and—most important—maintaining parallel skis throughout the turn. So effective was Seelos's maneuver that it enabled him to win slalom victories by ten seconds or more. Though Seelos's method was greeted coolly in Austria, it struck a responsive chord in France. Seelos was brought to Chamonix, where he coached the French team, then under the leadership of Emile Allais.

The then widely accepted Arlberg technique consisted of a wide windup rotation to get the skis to turn—it was a response to the loose connection between the skier and his skis. Allais solved all that by lashing his boots to the skis with leather thongs. Suddenly it was no longer necessary to twist the upper body to initiate a turn, since the legs, not the upper body, did the turning.

Allais further refined the parallel technique by adding a down-and-forward unweighting motion and a maneuver called the ruade, a lifting of the skis' tails in a horse-kick motion. It paid off. In 1939 the French swept the FIS World Championships—a feat, SKI reported, "that proves beyond any question of doubt that the French style of racing is the fastest yet devised."

Although Allais would not arrive in North America until after World War II, Canadian instructor Fritz Loosli was quick to recognize the potential of parallel skiing and proceeded to pave its way, in 1940, by proclaiming that "stem turns are a waste of time in learning to ski." So pervasive was Loosli's campaign for parallel skiing that Jack Miller, president of the Canadian Ski Instructors Alliance, a group staunch in their support of the Arlberg technique, made an about-face and publicly endorsed Loosli's system. It was the equivalent of a bombshell being thrown in the Canadian ski world. It was also all the impetus Loosli needed to establish a Parallel Instructors Association, whose aim, in Loosli's words, would be "to protect the ski public from unqualified opportunists."

Even while rotational skiing was at its zenith, and parallel was quickly catching on, a small group of Swiss and Austrian theorists were developing a system based on counterrotation—a twisting of the upper body in a direction opposite to the legs and skis. Despite the victories of Rudolf Rominger, who became the world's best slalom racer using the new technique, attempts made to institute the reverse-shoulder maneuver just before World War II were only marginally successful.

With the introduction of new techniques, and mounting skepticism about just how effectively they were being taught, the Eastern Amateur Ski Association directed that formal instructor-certifying procedures be established. The result was the first instructor certification exam, in 1938, administered at Suicide Six, Vermont. The failure rate was high—of seventeen instructors who took the exam, only six passed, causing certification chairman Ford Sayre to report that "many of those now giving instruction need further training in skiing as well as in teaching."

The idea of instructor certification spread quickly. Most skiers greeted the development positively, since before there was no unified system of ski instruction and anyone who could show a minimum level of competence in a specific system, and could explain it with reasonable clarity, was conferred with the reverential title of "ski instructor."

Wrote I. William Berry in *The Great North American Ski Book:*

> *Each system had its own strong advocates. Louis Cochand and Hans Georg had brought over the reverse shoulder. . . . [Fritz] Loosli was an early advocate of the all-parallel school of Emile Allais. [Hans] Thorner and [Walter] Prager taught traditional Swiss methods. Yet, despite these various heresies, Schneider's Arlberg method remained the accepted standard of what good ski technique was supposed to be. His personal lieutenants—[Luggi] Foeger, [Otto] Lang, [Friedl] Pfeifer, and [Benno] Rybizka—were not only superb skiers and teachers, but they were also highly articulate, and their message during this era of technique confusion was strongly supported by a number of influential American skiers.*

Right: *Rope tow 1, skier 0. The rope tow attracted hundreds of thousands of new skiers to the sport in the late thirties. Riding one took savvy, more than a modicum of athletic ability, and an appreciation of low comedy.*

Opposite, left: *The chair lift made its first appearance in the East in 1938 at Gunstock, New Hampshire. The 3,200-foot single-chair lift, as spectacular as it was, was matched in awe only by the ski area's 3,000-foot rope tow, which was ten times longer than any other in the world. Gunstock was the product of a federally funded work program developed under President Roosevelt during the Depression.*

Opposite, right: *The aerial tramway, introduced at Cannon Mountain, New Hampshire, in 1938, was the nation's first. It could haul two hundred skiers to the top in one trip. The tram was replaced in 1979 by a larger, four-million-dollar system that could carry five hundred skiers per trip. Cannon can legitimately claim other firsts: the country's first racing trail (the Taft, cut in 1929) and, nearby, the first ski school (Peckett's-on-Sugar Hill, 1930).*

If skiers of the day were in a quandary over proper technique, they were no less convinced of the prospect of making it through the winter without breaking a leg. In the thirties—in fact, for nearly half of the modern era of downhill skiing—the ski sport literally limped. Claims by the Red Cross notwithstanding ("Skiing," a spokesman huffed, "is about as dangerous as chess!"), if you skied long enough, you faced the reasonable certainty of severely spraining an ankle or breaking a leg. It was—given the rigid, unforgiving boot-to-ski fastenings of long thongs and, later, the down-pull Kandahar cable binding—an unfortunate fact of the times.

The first to do something about this fateful malaise was a Norwegian-born American named Hjalmar Hvam, who had gained fame as the best four-way (downhill, slalom, jumping, cross-country) skier in America before World War II. Hvam operated a rental shop at Mount Hood in Oregon, where he had ample opportunity to witness the fractured results of current bindings. It wasn't until 1937, when he broke his own leg as a result of a fateful cornice leap, that Hvam came upon a solution. While under ether as his leg was being mended, he had a dream, and when he awoke, he asked for a pencil and paper in order to sketch his idea: the complete principle of a releasing toe iron that would open when the foot was severely twisted. Hvam went on to build and market his binding—promoting it with the slogan "Hvoom with Hvam"—until the mid-sixties. By then more sophisticated designs had become popular—all of them based on Hvam's concept of twist-out release at the toe.

While Hjalmar Hvam was busy putting the sport back on its feet, another visionary, fifteen hundred miles away, was busy drilling it into the public consciousness.

© Trask

Fred Pabst, scion of the Milwaukee brewing family, discovered in 1933 that the beer business was not for him. A giant of a man and an accomplished collegiate ski jumper with a love for the outdoors, Pabst saw skiing as a sport, not just for the select few but for the masses. But the sport would never become popular, he knew, unless it was made easier—and that meant providing ski lifts. So Fred Pabst built mountains and ski lifts.

He started at Mont Saint Sauveur in the Laurentians of Quebec with an eighteen-hundred-foot rope tow that could haul fifty skiers at a time uphill. He installed and operated three more tows on adjacent hills, then headed south for New England.

Pabst invented a drag lift called the J-bar and erected four of them in New Hampshire, Vermont, and at Lake Placid, New York. He put up rope tows at areas he operated in Michigan and Minnesota. At one time, he owned seventeen ski areas, filling them with skiers by traveling from city to city and drumbeating the sport. He organized ski trains from Chicago, New York, and Boston, complete with restaurant and bar cars and live bands.

With World War II approaching, the crowds never materialized. Pabst abandoned his dream of a ski area conglomerate and focused his interests instead on Bromley, Vermont, which he opened in 1943.

If skiing for the masses fizzled as a concept in the prewar years, Pabst's legacy in another area still endures. One problem all ski areas of the time had to deal with was limited snow. Challenged by Hannes Schneider, who had shown at Mount Cranmore what slope clearing could do for ski teaching, Pabst plowed up his shrub-covered novice slope, re-moved stones, and laid down a bed of grass seed. The next winter, people were skiing on only four inches of snow—

Sparks-Moody-Hayes-Hollaus-Ruschp
Mansfield - 1940

manicured skiing had arrived. Area operators soon began flocking to Bromley to learn, and copy, what Pabst had started. Suddenly it was a whole new ball game.

With lifts, ski teaching systems, and a manageable snow surface now in place, people began to take skiing seriously. Just how seriously was demonstrated in the winter of 1943 by the Amateur Ski Club of New York in its appeal to the city's society editors: "The Amateur Ski Club of New York includes many wealthy and influential persons. Curiously enough, it is also devoted to skiing. News items about it, therefore, might fit more properly on sports rather than society pages." The New York City Ski Council, of which ASCNY was a member, also lobbied for standard terms for the reporting of ski conditions in the city's newspapers, recommending Fluffy, Slushy, and Sticky, among others.

Skiers of the time also started to take their clothing seriously. The sport, in fact, began to take on something of an "Alpine look." Included in a thirties skier's wardrobe might have been the following:

—Woolen "newsboy" cap (very trendy) or duckbill cap with "foreign legion" flaps to keep out snow and wind
—Reindeer sweater, de rigueur then, still popular today
—Collared shirt, worn buttoned, tie optional
—Gabardine jacket, very short, military in look
—Wool mitts, nattily patterned, sometimes warm, always wet, or "gauntlet" gloves to give a "snow warrior" impression and keep out snow and wind
—Wool knickers, preferably tweed, wide and baggy, worn with high socks to complete knicker look

Opposite: *Sepp Ruschp, major domo up front, and his "Fabulous Four" ski school at Mount Mansfield in Stowe, Vermont, 1940. From the rear: Kerr Sparks, Howard Moody, Lionel Hayes, Otto Hollaus, and Ruschp*

Right: *Okay, all together now—tips together, knees bent, tails apart. In the forties the Arlberg was alive and well at Mount Mansfield.*

—Baggy trousers in gabardine, always worn with belt, jacket, and sweater tucked in, best known for their flapping sound when coming down the slopes

No individual was more serious about, or did more to popularize skiing in the thirties and forties, than Lowell Thomas. The famous news commentator announced in 1940 that he would broadcast his regular Friday night program from Cannon Mountain, New Hampshire. Thomas, who first skied as a war correspondent with the Italian mountain troops in World War II, went on the air from other eastern resorts as well, always doing his utmost to give exposure to the sport he loved.

As he wrote of the skiing experience:

> The woods seem to fly past in a dizzy blur. The rush of wind whips tears from your eyes. No sport can match the freedom from earthbound plodding that you feel as you sail down a long straightaway. Muscles alert as a hair trigger, ready to shift balance with every change of slope, with each variation in snow. What a thrill is this mastery of muscles, what a zest in flirting with disaster at every bend in the trail. What does the skier think about in his mad career? He is tinglingly alive. Every nerve is tuned to the highest pitch. . . . A mountain scaled, and a trail run with the speed of the wind.

Though competition in the prewar era was confined for the most part to the big ski racing schools of the East—Dartmouth, Williams, Middlebury, the University of New Hampshire, Colgate, Syracuse, McGill—it was beginning to catch on at campuses elsewhere. Harvard, for example, having admitted rifle shooting as a minor sport, also accepted skiing.

One of the biggest events on the winter competition schedule was the Inferno, a ski race down the precipitous thousand-foot-high Headwall of Mount Washington's Tuckerman Ravine. It was here, in front of two thousand spectators, that a young downhiller named Toni Matt, an Austrian junior champion who had been cutting five, ten, sometimes thirty seconds off American course records, set a record that will probably never be beaten. The year was 1939, and Lowell Thomas described it this way:

> The first racers took a good three or four swinging high-speed turns on the Headwall to check their speed. But when Matt came bolting over the edge [because it was so steep, he knew a turn wouldn't slow him down], he schussed the wall like a lead plummet, hitting 85 miles per hour as he came streaming off the

bottom, his skis shattering the icy snow. Matt hit the Sherburne trail at timberline riding a fantastic head of speed, and the strain began to tell. The effort at each turn was increasingly exhausting. Finally, he hit the last S-turn; losing his grip on the snow, skis chattering, he went straight at a tree. But Matt gave a great, last-ditch scrambling lurch, missed the tree by a hair and blitzed across the finish. He was down in 6 minutes, 29.4 seconds, a full minute faster than the number two man, Dick Durrance. It was, and still is, the largest winning margin in the history of modern American skiing.

Matt, who went on to become U.S. National Downhill Champion in 1939 and 1941, was asked years later if there was any luck involved in his legendary schuss. "You're lucky," he said, "when you're nineteen, stupid, and have strong legs."

As the thirties drew to a close, the ski sport was revving up. There were now lift installations at Mount Rainier and Snoqualmie, Washington; Sun Valley, Idaho; Mount Hood, Oregon; Alta, Utah; Flathead National Forest, Montana; Jackson Hole and Medicine Bow, Wyoming; Winter Park, Berthoud Pass, and Pike's Peak, Colorado; Cisco, Snow Valley, Soda Springs, Sugar Bowl, and Yosemite, California; Bousquet, Massachusetts; Pico Peak, Stowe, Suicide Six, and Bromley, Vermont; Cannon Mountain, Mount Cranmore, Belknap (now Gunstock), and Hanover, New Hampshire; and Mont Tremblant, Quebec. Roger Langley, president of the National Ski Association, announced that there were a million skiers in the United States.

Opposite: *The Tyrol invades America. U.S. resorts drew the cream of Austria's instructor crop in the aftermath of World War II. Charming, spirited, party loving, these Sun Valley ski teachers—for whom the word gemütlichkeit seemed to have been invented—set a style that would carry American skiing into adulthood.*

Left: *Lowell Thomas in 1936, nattily attired in the uniform of the day. The world-renowned broadcaster, a driving force in skiing during his lifetime, sat on the boards of three New England ski resorts. In winter he broadcast nightly news shows from ski area base lodges, and—within a year of its introduction in the United States—he installed a rope tow at his estate in Pawling, New York.*

Below: *Fred Pabst (right)—inventor of the J-bar lift, founder of Bromley, Vermont, and one-time owner of seventeen ski areas—did more to promote skiing than anyone in his day. One of his more ceremonial roles at Bromley was handing out the race-day spoils, such as the annual Louise Orvis trophies that he, Mrs. Orvis, and Jack Ortlieb are shown awarding here.*

Along with skiing's rapid growth, however, had come a problem. With thousands of people of disparate skill careening down U.S. mountainsides every weekend, who would minister to the injured?

Enter Minnie Dole. Charles Minot Dole, a thirty-six-year-old insurance broker and ski buff from Greenwich, Connecticut, was skiing at Stowe, Vermont, when he fell, breaking his ankle. While his wife went for help, he lay in the snow—cold and wet, pain throbbing in his leg. When his rescuers arrived, they dragged Dole on his back down the trail, his injured leg riding on a piece of tin roofing. The break was so severe that his doctor doubted Dole would ever walk normally again.

"You'd think an accident such as this would have started me thinking along the lines . . . of a first aid organization," Dole later recalled in his book *Adventures in Skiing*. "But it took something even stronger to shake me out of the standard fatalism that skiers had at that time about accidents."

While on the mend, Dole learned that a close friend, Frank Edson, an inexperienced racer, had entered a downhill race, run into a tree on the edge of the course, and died. It was Edson's death, along with the memory of his own botched rescue at Stowe, that convinced Dole of the need for an organization that could administer on-the-spot aid to injured skiers. He campaigned for two years, and in 1938 the National Ski Association, recognizing the importance of Dole's work, asked him to set up a National Ski Patrol System. The NSPS now numbers more than 22,600 volunteers and professionals skilled in mountain rescue and first aid and dedicated to keeping the skier's day catastrophe free.

While Minnie Dole was busy organizing the National Ski Patrol, the National Ski Association was busy helping to fund Finland's war coffers. Said former U.S. president Herbert Hoover, in a letter to NSA president Roger Langley, "To winter-bound Americans, the thought of sportsmanship on the snow, its skill, its daring, brings a breath of fresh air to the minds even of the stay-at-home. In this bitter winter of war and exile it will hearten the kindred spirits of Finland to know of the generosity of our sportsmen who sympathize with those whose use of that sport must be put to the grim uses of defense."

Opposite, above: *A camouflaged Tenth Mountain Division trooper prepares for maneuvers. An elite corps, America's "Phantoms of the Snow" owed their existence to the persistence of Minnie Dole. Ivy Leaguers, ranchers, trappers, mule skinners, and Norwegian ski champions signed on with the Tenth and were sent to the Italian Apennines to help crack the Gothic Line. The Tenth's efforts eventually led to the capture of twenty thousand German soldiers.*

Opposite, below: *The Tenth Mountain Division on maneuvers at Camp Hale, Colorado. The Tenth also trained at Fort Lewis, Washington, near Mount Rainier. Veterans of the Tenth—an organization of four thousand members still active today—went on to launch Aspen Mountain, Loveland, Attitash, Vail, Mount Cranmore, White Pass, Arapahoe Basin, and many of America's other top ski resorts.*

The hit-and-run capability of the Finns in the Russo-Finnish war was impressive. During the winter of 1939–40, the Finns, with their mobility on skis, raided Soviet supply lines and brought the Russian army to a dead halt. It wasn't until spring, with the snow gone, that the Russians finally were able to overturn the Finnish resistance.

The Russians were nevertheless impressed. War Commissar Voroshiloff, urging Soviet youths to take up skiing, set a personal example by learning to ski himself. A Communist party organ of the time editorialized, "Tens of thousands of ski centers must be organized. Every Komsomol organization must teach boys and girls the technique of military action on skis. To skis, comrades!"

Another individual who was impressed with the Finns' use of skis in combat was the National Ski Patrol's Minnie Dole, who went to U.S. Army Chief of Staff General George C. Marshall and urged that if America should ever get involved in the war, it should have mountain troops—just in case.

General Marshall bought Dole's idea, ordered the formation of the Eighty-seventh Mountain Infantry Regiment at Fort Lewis, Washington, and Minnie Dole and his National Ski Patrol were given the task of recruiting twenty-five thousand men in sixty days to fill the regiment's ranks. Suddenly, for the first time in American military history, the army had a unit specializing in mountain and winter warfare.

As the Fort Lewis newspaper reported in 1942, "The army post has opened bids for 2,300 pairs of hickory skis, 2,300 sets of bindings, 2,300 pairs of poles, and 2,300 pounds of wax. Specifications call for the skis to be seven to seven-and-a-half feet in length and the wax to be provided in four-pound cans." A decision on boots was to come later. Early experiments with oversized-toe felt ski boots, nicknamed "Mickey Mouse Boots" by soldiers of the Eighty-seventh, were inconclusive. The boots worked well enough in cold, dry weather but were useless once they got wet.

The Eighty-seventh, which consisted of some of the finest skiers in the country, was soon expanded into the Tenth Mountain Division, headquartered at Camp Hale, Colorado. It was an elite corps, which by war's end would become the most highly decorated—and most casualty-ridden—division in World War II.

The Tenth got its first taste of action in the Aleutians in 1943 when it was sent to help regain the island of Kiska, then occupied by the Japanese. United States intelligence, however, had failed to learn that the Japanese had already departed. Casualties consisted of Americans accidentally shot by their own countrymen.

Pride for the Tenth nonetheless abounded. As SKI Magazine reported, "It is doubtful if any group will provide better material for our forces than will be found among skiers, for skiing has done much to fortify an important line of defense, namely our health. It has also taught us to be alert, to appreciate the true meaning of courage, given us the ability to suffer reverses, yet maintain the determination to come back tomorrow for victory."

Opposite: *Skiing on Mount Rainier in 1940. There were few crowds in the sport's early days, which was just as well for this hapless skier.*

Though skiing of the nonmilitary sort was held in check during the war, some skiers did manage to continue, and their activities were sometimes seen as unpatriotic. As one upstate New York newspaper reported, "Schenectady skiers, with slalom flags lashed to their car, had some difficulties last month with members of the Jehovah's Witnesses. Upon seeing the slalom flags on the car, they promptly told the skiers that they 'had better get out of town if they knew what was good for them.' "

Meanwhile, skiers, who weren't about to stand for such abuse, launched a counterattack on skiing's wartime critics. Wrote Alfred Sigal in SKI, "We raise our feeble voice to state our position before someone takes a potshot at skiing again. It is unfortunate that there is a minority group, sort of isolationists, who have had much to say about not skiing in wartime."

As for the resorts, most steered clear of the fray. Quebec's Château Frontenac, in its advertising, merely wished to remind the public that "A Week's Leave Is Long Enough To Learn To Ski!"

One result of America's entry into the war was the sudden depletion of the nation's ski instructors, most of whom had signed on for action with the Tenth. On the positive side, however, the shortage was a boon for the ladies. Under the SKI Magazine headline "Men Do Not Mind Taking Instruction From The Fair Sex" was this report: "Many ladies are proving that, contrary to predictions, men will not only accept, but really enjoy instruction from the female of the species—which should give encouragement to ski centers suffering from army-depleted ranks of teachers."

After the Kiska debacle, the Tenth trained for two more years and was then dispatched to Italy. The Germans were firmly entrenched in the Apennines, anchored atop Riva Ridge on the forbidding Mount Belvedere, a twelve-hundred-foot-high, nearly vertical rock ledge that blocked the entrance to the Po valley. By scaling Riva Ridge, whose face the Germans considered unclimbable, eight hundred members of the Tenth, equally at home climbing mountains as they were skiing down them, were able to surprise the Germans and take Mount Belvedere. The Tenth then charged ahead, overtaking one German stronghold after another. On April 23, 1945, the Tenth crossed the Po River, then chased German troops north toward the Brenner Pass. On May 2 the action in Italy ended with Germany's surrender.

The Tenth had been responsible for crippling or destroying nine German divisions. It also experienced an extraordinary number of casualties. Nearly a thousand members of the division never returned at the war's end, among them Torger Tokle, a ski jumper who had established a record unequaled in U.S. jumping history. Tokle was killed while leading an infantry platoon against the Germans in Italy.

The Tenth Mountain Division had brought together a group of men who would go on to establish the resorts, drumbeat the sport, popularize it as never before, and hatch a new era in American skiing.

PART II
FEISTY FORTIES, FABULOUS FIFTIES

Previous page: *Foreshadowing the do-your-own-thing mindset of the sixties, a Seattle skier of the forties tries a first descent off the roof of the Paradise Inn on Mount Rainier. It wasn't known whether he had lost his lift ticket, misplaced his room key and was trying to gain entry through his window, or was simply looking for fresh snow.*

The postwar years are certain to bring with them the greatest influx of skiers that this country has ever known.—SKI Magazine, 1945

Skiing, like all else in America in the postwar years, was returning, however begrudgingly, to normalcy. Sun Valley, after a two-and-a-half-year hitch as a wartime convalescence facility, returned to normal operations. The New York City Ski Council expressed alarm at the rising cost of a day's skiing as tow fees climbed from $1.00 to $1.50. Elsewhere, a technical journal reported, "Manmade snow, every bit as real as that which makes for a 'White Christmas,' has been produced in a cold chamber at General Electric research labs." Postwar Austria and Italy jumped back into the ski business with package tours that included "four meals daily totaling forty-five-hundred calories per day." French ski makers, hit by a hickory shortage, considered the use of plastics for ski construction. Canada's Laurentian Resorts Association, in a "Note to Single Men," reported that "on a typical weekend the ratio of gals to guys is often as high as four to one."

After the hibernation of its war years, skiing came back on the American scene like a Kansas twister, recharged with new energy and an unbridled spirit. In 1946 alone operators installed twenty-six new chair lifts or T-bars on U.S. mountainsides, including those at Mittersill, New Hampshire; Gore Mountain, New York; and Aspen, Colorado.

A former mining center whose inhabitants numbered some seventeen thousand during its heyday in the early 1890s, Aspen hit the skids in 1893 with the adoption of the gold standard and the collapse of the silver market. By 1936 the town was little more than a ranching community of two hundred. But investors, impressed by the development of Sun Valley, saw that Aspen, with an altitude that virtually guaranteed good snow depth, could be developed in the same way. A "boat tow," two four-passenger toboggans attached to a cable and pulled uphill by a rig from the defunct Little Annie mine, was built on Ajax Mountain; the Roch Run, named in honor of André Roch, an affable Swiss who had done much to bring skiing to Aspen in the prewar years, was cut; and Aspen, with a refurbished Gallagher's Saloon and Jerome Hotel, the only two establishments of note, opened for skiing in January 1938.

After the war, a young Tenth Mountain Division corporal named Friedl Pfeifer, who had discovered the superiority of Aspen's skiing during boot training at nearby Camp Hale, returned there to start the Aspen Skiing Corporation. In 1947 Pfeifer built the world's longest chair lift, 3,295 feet up the Roch. It was also the year that saw the introduction of a ski school and ski patrol in Aspen, the latter including another Tenth Mountain veteran, Pete Seibert, who went on to found Vail, Colorado, and Clif Taylor, who went on to invent the short-ski method of ski teaching.

In 1950 Aspen hosted the FIS Alpine World Championships. In the face of European strength—Austria swept all the women's events, the men's medals were captured by the Italians and the Swiss—the American team's performance wasn't so hot. Although Katy Rodolph and Andrea Mead took a fifth and sixth, respectively, in the downhill and slalom, the U.S.

The single chair lift on Ajax Mountain in Aspen, built in 1947, was then the world's longest.

team, as ski filmmaker John Jay put it, "offered more hospitality than competition." It was nevertheless an event that did much to enhance Aspen's image and establish it as one of the great ski centers. Another event that was to firmly establish Aspen was the arrival of Chicago industrialist Walter Paepcke. Paepcke, who gave up the sport after only a few tries, was to become one of skiing's greatest benefactors. As chairman of the Container Corporation of America, he envisioned his newfound Aspen as a place where the nations' leaders could be intellectually, physically, and spiritually revitalized, and he set about convincing his friends, also leaders in the business world, to invest in the town's development. Paepcke established the Aspen Company, which began restoring the historic town and led to the founding of the Aspen Institute, a center for the interaction of great minds in education, science, religion, and art. Pfeifer and Paepcke together were responsible for the rebirth of Aspen, a winter sports and culture capital whose reputation continues to grow to this day. With four mountains—Aspen Mountain, Buttermilk, Aspen Highlands, and Snowmass—Aspen is today the largest winter resort complex in the country and, to those skiers who have sampled her charms and continue to return, the mother lode of skiing in the United States.

Skiing took on a new glamour in the postwar years. People suddenly had a few dollars to spend and yearned to try the winter sporting life previously reserved for the adventurous rich. Resorts responded with the installation of new high-technology lifts. Equipment and technique, on the other hand, changed little in the years immediately following the war. For one thing, there was an abundant surplus of military ski equipment. Originally intended for the use of the Tenth Mountain Division, the gear was of remarkably high quality and was easily adaptable to the civilian sport. It was possible, in fact, to buy a pair of long, white army skis (of *splitkein* construction) and a baggy, but durable and warm, military suit for twenty-five dollars. Thousands did.

Thousands of other skiers, tired of burned hands and shredded gloves, also invested in "rope grippers." These devices, under trade names such as Safety-Grip, Tow Hold, Saf-T-Grip, and Rope Clutch ("the revolutionary tow gripper that will do the dirty work for you"), were a welcome antidote to the blistered palms and strained shoulders familiar to rope-tow riders of the era.

The postwar decade was a curious mix of status quo and experimentation. Though there was little difference between prewar and postwar racing techniques and the equipment used—new plastic ski bottoms, though exotic, had made little impression, and most skiers followed the traditional waxing ritual as before—the sport's theoreticians continued to experiment. They began to talk about a technique called *gegenschulter,* an adaptation of the reverse-shoulder technique

Aspen pre-Paepcke. The Chicago industrialist arrived in the fifties to resurrect the town, revitalize its spirit, and drumbeat to investors its potential as a winter sports and cultural center.

that allowed racers to get closer to a slalom gate. Although few instructors took it seriously, believing it was of absolutely no use to the recreational skier, *gegenschulter* did attract a fair number of proponents.

Whatever the fate of *gegenschulter,* most skiers of the time agreed that it was no longer sufficient merely to ski; the goal was to ski well. The ski instructor gained in stature. Impressed by an international tour by the amazing French national team in the late forties, American skiers embraced anything from France. A great debate raged between adherents of Hannes Schneider's Arlberg technique and the followers of Emile Allais's and Fritz Loosli's parallel system.

The 1948 Winter Olympics at Saint Moritz, Switzerland, the first in which downhill and slalom were recognized as separate events, also produced America's first gold-medal winner, Gretchen Fraser, who captured first in the slalom. Fraser went on to win silver in the ladies' combined. As spectacular as Fraser's performance was, it did not wholly overshadow an equally spectacular performance in the same season by an American fifteen-year-old named Andrea Mead, who had swept the combined honors at Pontresina, Switzerland. It was an achievement that would preface Mead's capture of two gold medals four years later at the Oslo Winter Games. The world of skiing had finally felt the impact of the American women.

As the fifties progressed, so did the sport. The decade saw the first ski flights to Europe. Boyne Mountain, Michigan, announced the opening of the Midwest's first chair lift as it transplanted the original lift from Sun Valley to its slopes. A challenge was issued by Frostie, Sun Valley's famous skiing dog, to "any and every skiing dog no matter what size, breed, or color to race in downhill or slalom on hickories, to be solely manipulated by said dog." The canine challenge, unfortunately, never came off. Roland Palmedo—Wall Streeter, aviator, mountain climber, kayak expert, world traveler, and all-around adventurer—announced the development of Mad River Glen, Vermont. Insurance bigwig C. V. Starr unveiled plans for a resort on Mount Mansfield in Stowe, Vermont. Kingfield storekeeper Amos Winter led the descent of the first group of skiers down the flanks of Sugarloaf Mountain in Maine. Alec Cushing announced the opening of Squaw Valley, California. And Walt Schoenknecht startled the world with his discovery of artificial snow.

Schoenknecht, a lanky, crew-cut World War II veteran and inveterate skier, had opened Mohawk Mountain in northern Connecticut in 1947. He had six rope tows, a base lodge . . . and no snow. Determined that Mother Nature would not get the upper hand, Schoenknecht trucked in blocks of ice, crushed it, and scattered it on the slope. But that took time, the surface didn't last for long, and ice was expensive. So Schoenknecht looked for other solutions.

A solution appeared two years later when the Tey Manufacturing Company, makers of aluminum skis, came to Schoenknecht with a problem of their own: if the resorts couldn't guarantee snow, there would no longer be a market for skis. Schoenknecht threw it back in their lap, suggesting they put their best engineering minds on the problem, which they did. Presto—using a combination of hoses, nozzles, air compressors, and water, the first artificial snow was produced.

No sooner had Schoenknecht finished laying the world's first manmade snow on the trails at Mohawk than he trained his gaze north, to Vermont. There he bought acres of mountainous farmland and sold public shares to build Mount Snow. Said Schoenknecht in his *Mount Snow Newsletter,* "We have an unusual setup in that our area with its thousand-dollar shares of stock is not only built by skiers, but owned by skiers. Your shares in Mount Snow provide what amounts to a

Right: *Stein Eriksen, age nineteen, at the 1950 FIS Alpine World Championships, shows the style that would earn him two gold medals in the 1952 Oslo Winter Olympics and a place in the heart of an adoring American public.*

Below: *The Swiss, Swedish, and Norwegian ski teams gather for opening ceremonies at the 1950 FIS World Championships in Aspen. Though the opening ritual was a far cry from the spectacular ceremonies orchestrated today, the events were no less historical—it was the first time for a world Alpine ski championship in North America.*

Left: *Austria's Christian Pravda in action in the 1950 World Championships. One of ski racing's most enduring competitors, Pravda won the Austrian national downhill championship nine times, Sun Valley's prestigious Harriman Cup three times, then went on to become a top pro on the U.S. circuit.*

lifetime of skiing." Schoenknecht eventually sold 240 shares by panhandling them in the lift line. It was enough to get Mount Snow started.

Schoenknecht—impetuous, excitable, with boundless energy and imagination—innovated in other ways: trail design, for instance. While others continued to cut circuitous, narrow trails, Schoenknecht carved his wide and in the fall line, creating the kind of superior ski experience found at modern resorts today. He also built the first outdoor heated swimming pool in the East, a complete medical facility, and linked Mount Snow's base lodge by cable car to the resort's hotel. Schoenknecht had other plans, some of which were destined to remain dreams and little more. There was, for example, the idea of a glass-enclosed base village and a vast outdoor amphitheater "for entertainment on a grand scale," to be created by exploding a nonpolluting type of atom bomb. Fraught by frustration and financial setbacks, Schoenknecht, in a dust-to-dust scenario played out by visionaries and entrepreneurs of other eras, eventually sold his beloved Mount Snow and returned to where he had started, Mohawk Mountain, a resort that he continues to operate today.

Amenities such as those that Walt Schoenknecht could provide were what the postwar skier wanted. And resorts responded—with better food, better lodging, high-capacity, high-speed lifts, and groomed slopes. It was the latter— neatly manicured, more manageable snow surfaces—that did more than anything else to attract the new skiers.

For years skiers were forced to put up with ice, crud, bumps, and other assorted hostile forms of skiing impedimenta. Trail packing, by foot, was an arduous, time-consuming exercise and not many resorts cared to do it.

Enter Steve Bradley, father of the Bradley Packer, a giant gravity-operated device that could make interstate-smooth highways out of corduroy trails. Bradley, one of seven sons of a Wisconsin doctor, was hardly the type to run a ski area. Although he had been born into a skiing family and had ski raced for Dartmouth, he had planned to become an art professor. By his own admission a self-styled "ham actor, dubious motion picture magnate, and artist of no renown," Bradley once wrote, "Manage a ski area? Not me. Mine was to be the quiet life, on a university campus, dedicated to the development of significant attitudes among young men and women." But he was invited, after an impressive officiating performance at the 1950 World Championships at Aspen, to become area manager at Winter Park, Colorado.

Winter Park, like other ski areas of the day, had a mogul problem. The problem was that once area workers beat the moguls down with shovels they popped up elsewhere on the mountain. Bradley, frustrated with the time required daily to deal with the moguls, came upon the solution: a grooming machine, in this case a grooming machine powered by simple gravity, its rate of descent controlled by someone skiing before it.

Bradley's first grooming machine was a large four-hundred-pound slatted wooden roller and blade at the front of which a ski patrolman could position himself to steer it down the hill. It was an odd-looking contraption, more Erector set than engineering marvel, but it worked beautifully. It not only chopped the tops off moguls but could pack the snow after a fresh snowfall for a more consistent skiing surface. Simple but effective, Bradley's packer was the forerunner of the giant $150,000 diesel-powered groomers used for custom surfacing of U.S. ski trails today.

With the advent of machine grooming and artificial snow, things were getting serious. How serious was reflected in the pages of some sixty-one ski books available by 1953 to help a skier master his moves and bring more fun and finesse to his outings. Six books alone were written by the venerable and prolific Sir Arnold Lunn, conceiver, creator, and one-man lobby for the slalom, an event that would change the world of ski racing forever.

Recreational skiers were also getting serious. In New York, for example, more than 100,000 skiers used the state's ski areas in 1953. The average expenditure by the New York skier for travel, lodging, meals, lifts, and equipment during the season was $98, which totaled nearly $10 million spent by skiers in New York alone. It was also disclosed that each New York skier had an average investment of $92 in skis, boots, poles, and clothing.

Some skiers, consumed by their new enthusiasm and believing there might be a financial bonanza to be made in the sport, even thought about starting their own ski resorts. Many had read Mad River Glen owner Roland Palmedo's missive in SKI entitled "How to Plan a Ski Area," learned about the elements necessary for a successful resort—proper terrain, orientation, snowfall, altitude, accessibility, housing, financing, types of lifts, trail design—and then called it quits.

Then there were a skier's equipment concerns. These were serious, too—going through a season without basketless poles, loose screws, warped skis, and spongy soles required great preparation. Skiers took pains to learn more about their equipment. They discovered air-cell ankle supports, the first idea in inflatable boots. The ingenious invention of a Saint Anton bootmaker, they were simply inserted between the inner and outer boot, laced up, then inflated with a bicycle pump until they were tight. Skiers also learned about new bindings, such as the Hanson, a heel-release system marketed by the Miller Ski Company with the claim that they would give any skier $500 who "will follow us through the same falls at the same speed, using any other standard type of binding, without sustaining injuries."

Opposite, below: *Andrea Mead Lawrence, American ski racing phenomenon. In 1948, at age fifteen, she won the combined at Pontresina, Switzerland. Three years later she won the Hahnenkamm downhill at Kitzbühel, Austria. One year later she skied to two gold medals at the 1952 Oslo Winter Olympics. It was a feat no other American has ever accomplished.*

Some skiers weren't so serious. The "ski bum," for one, was coming into his own as one of the sport's more colorful characters. Commenting on this new breed in a 1948 story headlined "Ski Bums Wait Tables, Ogle Heiresses," SKI Magazine reported:

> *The professional skier is understood. Ostensibly, he skis to eat. But the Ski Bum is beyond all this. He eats to ski—all else is secondary. He pursues the snow with a passion that amounts to monomania. Yet when the question of why he skis is put to a relatively articulate Ski Bum, he will at first exhibit all manner of reactions and provide platitudinous answers.*
>
> *Further questioning, beyond the health-exhilaration stage, produces the answer of last resort, delivered in a tone of finality: "I ski to have fun." And the implication is that if one persists in this sort of philosophical heckling, one will get a stein of beer in one's kisser.*

One topic of conversation that was common even to ski bums of the period was the earlier-mentioned *gegenschulter*. The much talked-about technique, no longer considered a stylistic aberration, blossomed in the early fifties and was practiced by most of the world's best racers and a good many advanced recreational skiers as well.

The graceful, rhythmic movements of *gegenschulter* were finally endorsed with the introduction of the New Official Austrian Ski Technique in 1955. Its ultimate form, called wedeln (a continuous turning down the fall line), became a rage after SKI's introduction of the technique to American skiers—demonstrated blasphemously in its pages by an American, Brooks Dodge. That winter every ski school taught wedeln.

Though wedeln was considerably more complex than the older rotation pioneered by Hannes Schneider and his disciples, it took the ski world by storm. The reasons were several, but the most important reason was that its introduction coincided with that of the metal ski.

The metal ski, a product of the fifties, was simply far easier to turn than older wooden skis. The earliest metal skis to be marketed commercially were the Dow Metal Air Ski and the Truflex (née Alu 60), the latter developed by the Chance-Vought Aircraft Company. Because their bare metal bases would not hold wax and the skis would occasionally take an unwanted permanent shape, skiers considered them "tin cans" and refused to buy them.

Meanwhile, an aviation engineer by the name of Howard Head—a 6-foot-4-inch Baltimore bon vivant with early aspirations of being a creative writer but who instead discovered himself to be "embarrassingly good at structural design"—had gone skiing for the first time at age thirty-two. It was in 1946, the area was Stowe, Vermont, and Head, after a marvelous day "but with lots of falls," discovered that "skiing was my sport."

Below: *Mount Snow's monorail lift was a conversation piece of its day. Things had come a long way since America's first rope tow in 1934.*

Opposite, above: *Sun and camaraderie have always been two of the sport's great attractions. These skiers enjoy both on the deck of the base lodge at Stowe, Vermont.*

Opposite, below left: *Lift lines, like this one in Vermont, became synonymous with skiing in the forties.*

Opposite, below right: *Stowe's Octagon, still purveying food and shelter, served as a welcome warming hut for Mount Mansfield skiers who braved the blustery, often bone-chilling ride to the top.*

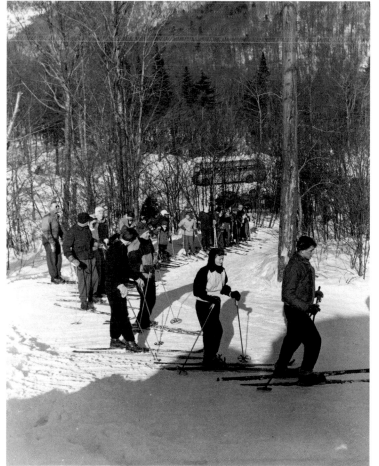

Below: *Despite the growing popularity of lifts, not all forties skiers were ready to give up the hearty, sweat-inducing climb that earned them the right to a downhill run. The herringbone, still part of the cross-country skier's uphill repertoire, is seldom needed by the Alpine skier today.*

Opposite: *The ruade, introduced by Frenchman Emile Allais as a skis-parallel alternative to the Arlberg technique, was characterized by an explosive unweighting. The maneuver was accomplished by pressing the knees forward and hopping, the ski tips serving as a pivot point for the turn.*

Below: *Howard Head (at rear) examines a pair of new Head skis with Walter Haensli, Head's European distributor in the fifties, at Head's Timonium, Maryland, factory. By 1957 Head had produced 27,000 ("on the way," said Head, "to 100,000") pairs of skis. The Head Standard and Master models sold for $85 to $125. It was then a pretty stiff price to pay, but the world lined up to buy them.*

Opposite: *Amazing grace. Stein Eriksen—handsome, dashing, blond—embodied the special spirit of American skiing, fifties style. To ski "Stein's way"—hip-angulated, reverse-shoulder, squeezed-knees parallel—became a national obsession.*

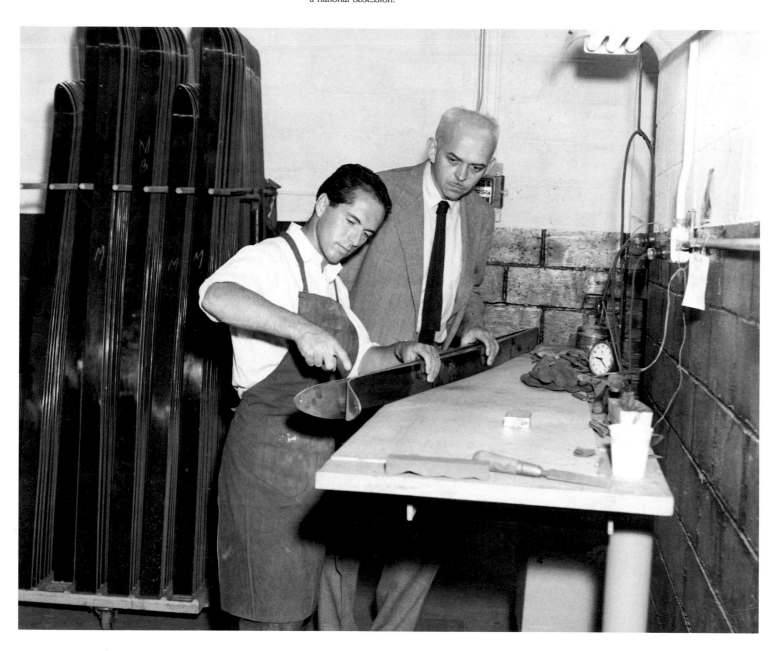

Eriksen then came to the United States to teach America to "Ski Like Stein," which in fact became the goal of most skiers of the day. So elegant, so inspiring was Eriksen on snow that he was turned into an instant idol, a hero who mesmerized men and lifted the hearts of women. "All Stein needed to do was enter a room," said Martie Sterling, a former lodge owner remembering Eriksen's early days in Aspen. "Eyes glazed. Tongues tied. And when he swooped down the ski hills, the 'aaaaaahs' rose like dawn over Mandalay."

Eriksen's style of skiing was sheer beauty, a graceful legs-together technique that was glorious to see. Equally glorious to see were Eriksen's spectacular airborne somersaults. His secret? He had trained in gymnastics as a child, and like many Norwegian youngsters he thought nothing of performing somersaults off a jump. Later, he reported that he and his friends had started flipping during World War II as a substitute for racing—they refused to compete against the German occupation troops.

Recalled Martie Sterling of Eriksen's magical weekly performances at Aspen Highlands, "He would give a wave to the crowd, roar down the course, hit the jump, stretch into a swan, turn over in midair, and land to thunderous applause."

Eriksen's spellbinding stunts would later set the stage for freestyle skiing. But for now, his balletic magic and graceful turns were what thrilled thousands of skiers and launched the sport into a period of explosive growth in the mid-1950s.

And there to capture it all—Eriksen at his somersaulting best, deep powder skiers, stunting, racing, high jinks on skis—were the filmmakers. Ski movies, of course, were not entirely new. German filmmaker Dr. Arnold Fanck had produced the first ski movie of note in 1921. It was called *Der Weisse Rausch* (retitled *The Ski Chase* in English) and it showed Hannes Schneider and pals climbing and skiing the deep powder of Austria's Arlberg. When in the thirties American interest moved from jumping to Alpine skiing, a new era in ski filmmaking was born. Among those in the forefront was San Francisco dentist Dr. Frank Howard, who pioneered with the first color ski films. Stowe's Victor Coty, an inveterate skier-outdoorsman, showed films that still delight Mount Mansfield skiers today. John Jay, who popularized the lecture-film circuit, went on to narrate his ski films for forty-five years. Otto Lang, a Hannes Schneider disciple and former Sun Valley ski school director, premiered his film *Ski Flight* alongside Walt Disney's *Snow White and the Seven Dwarfs* at Radio City Music Hall. And Warren Miller, who also got his start in the Sun Valley ski school, still holds the unchallenged record of nearly forty consecutive annual ski film productions, many narrated by Miller and all produced using a mix of derring-do, thrills, and laughs.

It was also the era of Mitch Cubberley's Cubco, the first cableless "step-in" binding. An elegantly simple system with release springs at the toe and heel, it was to become one of the most popular bindings of its time. So what if its boot plates

Opposite: *Eriksen, headed for a rare spill, attempts to make the best of a bad situation. Such acrobatics came naturally to Eriksen, whose airborne somersaults became legendary.*

Below: Sun Valley Serenade *did more to popularize Sun Valley than the stars who flocked to the Idaho resort every winter. In this scene comedian Milton Berle prepares to show Sonja Henie, the film's star, a thing or two.*

made walking on icy parking lots risky, or if a tap in the lift line would cause you to come loose from your skis? The Cubco was, as Mitch Cubberley claimed so convincingly, "for skiers who have to work on Mondays." Also introduced during the period were the Kofix plastic ski base and the Henke Speedfit, the world's first buckle boot. Small wonder the specialty ski shop flourished—the purveying of ski equipment became big business.

On the resort side, Dave McCoy christened Mammoth Mountain, California, with a permanent rope tow. Ernie Blake made his first forays by Cessna into the mountains of New Mexico to map development of Taos Ski Valley. Sun Valley packaged the nation's first "ski weeks." Steamboat, Colorado, produced, in seventeen-year-old Buddy Werner, the first American male to win a major European downhill race—the Holmenkollen-Kandahar in 1954. America's first Pomalifts, fanny-platters whose through-the-legs tow bar earned them the sobriquet "skier's birth-control device," were installed at

Arapahoe Basin, Colorado; Snow Ridge, New York; and Suicide Six, Vermont. The suggestion box at Mad River Glen, Vermont, was discovered to have no bottom and a wastebasket underneath. The average price of a daily lift ticket had climbed to $2.90.

There were also reports that European ski manufacturers were scrambling to match Howard Head's revolutionary "metal-plastic-wood 'sandwich' ski, which has proved very tasty indeed," and first mentions were made of a revolutionary stretch pant.

Prior to 1936 the words "ski apparel" had not appeared in the skier's vocabulary. Most skiers of the day dressed in whatever worked. But whatever worked wasn't necessarily fashionable—big puffy parkas, knickers, riding breeches, or baggy pants that tucked into socks and made flapping sounds as the skier descended the slope. What was needed was a real skier look, something sleek and sexy that would at the same time keep the skier warm and dry.

Three firms—Slalom Skiwear, Sun Valley Ski Clothing Company, and White Stag—sold ski apparel in the thirties. The major producer was Harold Hirsch, a Dartmouth graduate whose family had built an outdoor clothing business from its foundings as a purveyor of sails for deep water sailing ships, tarpaulins, deck awnings, cordage, tents, and sea bags. Hirsch's clothing line, which he called White Stag (from an inverted English translation of the original company name, Hirsch-Weiss), caught on quickly with skiers. At the same time, another Dartmouth graduate, Lew Russfield of the Sun Valley Ski Clothing Company, had created his own line of ski apparel. He used gabardine to give his designs a "trim look" that reflected contemporary fashion trends. They were marked by a rakish inverted-triangle appearance, moving downward from smooth, sometimes padded shoulders to slim taut-drawn ankles. Though Russfield and Hirsch were competitors, they agreed on one thing—some kind of stretch fabric was needed in order to meet the demands of both function and fashion. Hirsch tried a Swiss material combining wool and Lastex, but it couldn't be dry cleaned. Russfield tried a French elasticized stretch material, but it couldn't be ironed. Frustrated, both sat back and waited for someone else to come up with an answer.

Another, in Europe, didn't bother to wait. Willy Bogner and his wife, Maria, living in Munich, were shown a new fabric made of wool and a new Swiss nylon called Helanca, which could be pulled any which way and still return to its original shape. Adapted to the wearer's body, it was tailored, sexy, and because of its wool content, warm.

Although the new material was difficult to tailor, Maria experimented, and Willy tested, and by 1952 they had something. That ski season Willy and Maria introduced the new stretch pant and the clamor began. By 1955 the Bogners began offering their designs in bright, nontraditional colors, all selling for the unheard-of price of forty dollars and up. As SKI reported, "Racers, who once wrapped thongs around their pants to prevent them from flapping, switched to stretchies.

*Scenes like this, below Herman Saddle
on Mount Baker, Washington, were
common in the northern Cascades in
the forties. Note that turns of longer
arc—in some cases, no arc—were
favored.*

Marilyn Monroe, Ingrid Bergman, and the Shah of Iran wore them. Henry Ford ordered fifteen pairs. Overnight, skiing had
been transformed into a sexy and very visible sport.''

   Skiing was on the threshold of a glamorous new age. With the coming of stretch pants, the sport was suddenly given a
whole new look—slim, sexy, fast. Fashion became an integral part of skiing and skiing an integral part of American life. The
sport settled on the American consciousness with a decided air of elegance.

The promise of beauty, challenge, and the great outdoors lured many Americans in the forties to mountains big and small. Mount Baker, Washington

PART III
SKIING GOES BIG TIME

Previous page: *For some, finding skis after a warming break in the base lodge was tough work. For others, just getting beyond the ski rack with skis on was a problem. Jay Peak, Vermont*

Opposite: *Precision, like the close-order drill demonstrated at the Jay Peak ski school, has always been at the core of a professional ski teacher. The threesome trailing in this photo had not yet mastered the art.*

If the forties and early fifties were formative for skiing, the period 1956–65 marked the boom era of the sport. Suddenly, everything was big time: mere ski hills were now "resorts," America became a ski racing power (sort of), advances in equipment abounded, and special interest groups sprang up like tadpoles in a stream. Things were really getting organized.

The Austrian influence, for all the impact the North Americans had had upon the sport, was still present. Toni Sailer, winning an unprecedented three gold medals in the 1956 Winter Olympics, followed two years later with a three-out-of-four-medal sweep at the World Championships. He led Anderl Molterer, Toni Spiess, Christian Pravda, Othmar Schneider, and Ernst Hinterseer—an Austrian ski racing machine that one ski historian later called the "Dallas Cowboys of Downhill."

Experimentation in the "proper technique" continued. French theoreticians Jean Vuarnet and Georges Joubert published a book showing that the secret ingredient of the new racing technique was a shortening of the ski turn by starting it, of all things, with a skid. Vuarnet, along with fellow Frenchmen James Couttet and Paul Gignoux, later went on to develop a more natural skiing style called Christiania léger, in which the body remained square over the skis. Doug Pfeiffer, an instructor at Snow Summit, California, thought America's preoccupation with formal technique silly and began his School for Exotic Skiing, teaching and promoting Tip Thrusts, the Flying Sitz, the Deep-crotch Christy, the Outrigger, and other fancy moves. "What we're trying to do," said Pfeiffer, "is put the fun back into skiing." American skiers, still hooked on wedeln, found the spelling of the maneuver equal to its complexity. SKI's readers wrote: "It's hard to learn wedlyn from a magazine.... The articles on welding are great! ... Widdling is wonderful!"

Equipment experimentation, meanwhile, continued apace, and the debate over wood versus metal skis was confused further by the introduction of fiberglass. By 1961 five manufacturers—Rossignol, Sailer, Plymold, Kneissl, and Veneko— had introduced fiberglass skis, basically hickory laminates wrapped in a fiberglass skin. SKI published its first feature on the new synthetic skis, listing Kneissl's White Star ski under both epoxy and fiberglass, which showed how much anyone knew about the new material.

But the big news, the one development that did more to bring new comfort, convenience, and performance to skiing, was the plastic boot. Henke, a Swiss boot manufacturer, had introduced the Speedfit, the world's first buckle boot, in 1955. Suddenly it was no longer necessary to spend frustrating minutes fumbling with icy fingers over contrary laces. As wondrous as the new boot was, however, it did have one flaw: the force exerted by the buckles tended to deform not only the leather but the foot within.

Mastery of the uphill climb was part of the introduction to the Arlberg technique. There were always, of course, those spoilsports who said the heck with it and preferred to turn their backs on it all. Jay Peak, Vermont

Enter Bob Lange, a Harvard mechanical engineering student who recognized the miserable inefficiencies of the leather ski boot—low, soft, and with the propensity to stretch at least two sizes on a wet day. While Lange knew that forward flex was desirable in a ski boot, to make the linkage between skier and ski more precise he believed that the boot should also be laterally rigid and high enough to permit the lower leg, rather than the ankle, to edge the ski.

As with most inventions in skiing, Bob Lange's idea of a ski boot came about because of personal frustration. Although he had been a strong college swimmer, he had weak ankles. And like most skiers of the time, it had taken him most of a season to progress from the stem.

After college, Lange went into the family insurance business back home in Dubuque. He was also fascinated with plastics, so he started a plastics fabrication firm and began making all kinds of gadgets—kiddie cars, refrigerator interiors, Hula-Hoops.

The idea of a plastic ski boot—particularly after seeing what Howard Head had done in building skis using nontraditional materials—obsessed Lange. Finally, in 1957, after months of experimentation, Bob Lange had his first plastic ski boot, created from vacuum-molded ABS Royalite plastic. "After only two turns," he said, "I knew I had a boot better than anything ever made before." A lace-up design in blue and white, it held its shape but was so stiff that it took two men to lace it, and in very cold weather the boot cracked. "We made 750 pairs the first year," Lange reminisced, "and fifty percent of them broke." Lange later added a hinge to the boot for increased forward flexing, switched to a less heavy du Pont polyurethane plastic for better performance, and added buckles, a real advantage in closing the stiff plastic shell. Within ten years millions of skiers would put their feet in Lange boots.

While Bob Lange was ushering in the "era of the boot," other things were happening. There were 78 ski areas and 104 lifts in the United States in 1956. Mad River Glen's Roland Palmedo warned the ski industry against overexpansion but to no avail—ten years later there were 662 areas and 1,496 lifts. The Midwest built its third chair lift, Michigan's Boyne Mountain installed the world's first triple chair, and Wildcat, New Hampshire, opened with America's first gondola. *Today's Health* magazine claimed that "skiing is less dangerous than football or boxing." Austrian Hans Gmoser helicoptered his first skiers into the Canadian Rockies, touching off the "heli-skiing" craze. Canada's Lucille Wheeler won downhill and giant slalom gold and America's Sally Deaver won giant slalom silver in the 1958 World Championships. Austria's Sepp Kober arrived at The Homestead in West Virginia to build the South's first real ski area in 1959. SKI reported that "elasticized stretch pants are a way of life, and anyone without them may be considered gauche." In 1962 more than half of all skis sold were still made of wood. American skiers began grousing about the price of a lift ticket, which went from an average $3.10 in 1956 to $3.99 in 1963. And the Professional Ski Instructors of America proceeded to formulate

The Graduated Length Method of ski in-struction, pioneered by Clif Taylor, used increasingly longer ski lengths as the skier improved. Refined, polished, and promoted by ski schools through-out the country, GLM could turn never-evers into skiers in a single day. Jerry Muth (opposite), former Vail ski school director, was an early booster of GLM. (Beginners in the shortest-length skis were not required to ski with their bind-ing's toe canted sideways.)

the American Ski Technique—snowplow, snowplow turn, stem turn, stem christie, parallel turn—to create a uniform system of teaching and enable the skier to move from ski school to ski school without missing a beat in his progress.

If American ski teaching was finally getting organized, it certainly wasn't apparent to the rest of the world. In 1962 the Americans participated for the first time in Interski, the quadrennial conclave of the world's top instructors, who demonstrate in elegantly choreographed and synchronized maneuvers their latest approaches to ski teaching and ski technique. Reported SKI in October 1962, "The U.S. team was the least disciplined outfit. Since there is no American style, they were demonstrating with superb honesty what is really a fact—that American ski teachers do not ski alike."

No matter—America finally had its own "technique." But Clif Taylor wasn't convinced. He had a few ideas of his own. And they were not tied to the prewar Arlberg technique and the insistence that the proper length for a ski was the height of the skier's upstretched arm.

In 1955 Taylor, a certified ski instructor, arrived at Hogback, at the time home to a clan of eccentric Vermonters who insisted on skiing with the tails of their seven-foot skis sawed off. Taylor was convinced his new disciples were right—that all that was needed to cut the hellishly long time needed for a person to learn to ski was to put them on short skis.

Taylor's first step was purposely to design a short ski, not just a cut-down long one. His fledgling success was a five-foot ski with straight sides. But this, he felt, was still too long. A skier could turn with even less effort on a shorter pair, so Taylor arranged to make a thirty-two-inch ski, which he called the "Shortee."

Taylor traveled to thousands of ski shops to sell his ski. He also went to ski schools, and when that didn't work he opened a school of his own. He even persuaded newscaster Lowell Thomas to switch to Shortees. Taylor's success in teaching with short skis was not without its effect. Ten years later, in 1965, SKI's editors, impressed with Taylor's knack in getting problem learners to ski, sent fifty pairs of Taylor's Shortees to Killington, Vermont; Boyne Mountain, Michigan; and Mont Tremblant, Quebec, to test the skis in a learning situation. One idea that emerged was to start beginners on short skis, then "graduate" them, in Taylor's words, to longer skis as they progressed. In experiments the following winter, Clif Taylor's theory—that people taught on short skis learned faster—was proved and a new method of teaching, the Graduated Length Method (GLM), was launched. Over the next decade thousands of unathletic hopefuls would take up the sport.

Meanwhile, experimentation with technique continued. Counterrotation and angulation replaced rotation as an advanced maneuver. In an abandoned New Jersey steel mill, an inventor by the name of Ray Hall designed a new learning slope, a wide pulley-powered treadmill called the Ski Dek, still in use today.

In fashion, the mod look was in. Quilted nylon parkas, worn longer, moving the emphasis from the waist to the legs, were the rage, as were stretch pants, tight and bright and still worn in the boot, to emphasize a skier's sultry, muscular leg.

Although the wool pom-pom hat was promoted by manufacturers, most skiers—males, at least—preferred the wool headband; it covered the ears while letting the hair flow stylishly free. For women, the Flip, a hairstyle that went heavy on the hair spray, was popular. The cotton turtleneck, for layering under sweaters and to highlight the "skier tan," was a part of every skier's wardrobe.

No single event did more to bring exposure to the sport of skiing in America than the 1960 Squaw Valley Winter Olympics. Telecast to millions of American homes, the Games were the brainchild of Alexander Cushing, cofounder with Wayne Poulsen of Squaw Valley, California. Cushing's campaign to get the Winter Games was intended more to attract publicity for his resort than as an earnest Olympic bid. "I had no more interest in getting the games," Cushing later confessed, "than the man in the moon." But when news of Squaw's candidacy reached the public, Cushing was bombarded with mail. "I got letters from people saying what a nice thing I was doing," he said, "and it made me feel bad." So Cushing waged an all-out campaign in 1954 to bring the Games to Squaw Valley, then with only a chair lift, two rope tows, and a lodge. Technically, it was not even a town.

Cushing's impressive performance before the International Olympic Committee, with scale model of the proposed Olympic site and all, won him the Games by a narrow 32–30 second-ballot vote, edging out Innsbruck, Austria. Avery Brundage, the feisty IOC chairman, was flabbergasted. "Cushing," he warned, "you're going to set the Olympic movement back twenty-five years!" On the contrary, Cushing later recalled, "We won the Games with a purely intellectual

Alec Cushing (right) campaigned for the 1960 Winter Olympics to bring attention, and skiers, to his new resort, Squaw Valley, which wasn't even a town. Cushing beat out giant Innsbruck for the Games, a fact that, coupled with the misfortunes of the Austrian team at Squaw, did not endear him to the Tyrol. Pounded by blizzards right up until opening day, the Squaw Valley Games (below) began with brilliant sun and attendant showmanship. The first televised Winter Olympics in the United States, the 1960 Games sparked a boom in American skiing interest.

Left: *Squaw Valley Olympic slalom action*

Below: *The 1960 U.S. Ski Team included Tom Corcoran, Betsy Snite, and Penny Pitou. Can you find them?*

Below left: *Austria's Anderl (the Blitz from Kitz) Molterer was an overpowering presence on any course—amateur or pro. An uncompromising perfectionist, during the period 1952–62 he placed first in more international races than any other male competitor. Among his two hundred first-place finishes were four wins in the Hahnenkamm downhill, eleven Austrian national championships, and three world pro championships. A native of Kitzbühel, Austria, Molterer moved to the United States in 1959 and settled in Aspen, where he owns a ski shop today.*

Below right: *Tom Corcoran, one of America's top male skiers in the late fifties, competed on two Olympic teams (1956, 1960) and won just about every national title of his day. Raised in the Laurentians of Quebec, schooled at Dartmouth, coached by Walter Prager and Emile Allais, he is the founder and owner today of Waterville Valley, New Hampshire.*

Bottom left: *Canada's Ann Heggtveit ripped down the Squaw Olympic slalom course in fifty-four seconds flat. For someone who had won the central Canadian senior women's combined at age eight (the leading skier fell) a gold medal was not an unexpected feat.*

Austria's Karl Schranz (below) was the racer that other racers gunned for in the sixties. Schranz was touted as Killy's archrival. Until he lost to Killy in the 1968 Olympics, he claimed that the French star and his teammates were "overrated."

idea: the Olympics had become top-heavy and there was a need to return to simplicity. That was my approach. It shows the power of ideas, particularly when we had nothing else."

Nothing is not exactly what Squaw was blessed with on the days prior to the opening ceremonies. In fact, a Sierra snowstorm of blizzard proportions hit, threatening to ruin the events. But Cushing's luck held, the sun came out minutes before Walt Disney's elaborately orchestrated opening ceremony, the obligatory doves were released, San Francisco and Reno society hostesses scrambled to see who could snare the most important visitors for their parties, and cloudless skies, pageantry, and a holiday spirit lasted to the end of the Games. Everyone was joyous.

Everyone except the Austrians. It may well have started with the controversy over the viability of Squaw Valley's downhill course. "One long schuss and two turns," complained Austria's Christian Pravda. "A fair test," replied Cushing.

Whatever the reason, the result was that the unbeatable Austrians could win no more than a single gold medal—Ernst Hinterseer in the slalom.

It was demoralizing enough to see their ski racing fortunes plundered by the Swiss and the Germans and the French. Worse, the *North Americans,* of all ski racing's traditional nonpowers, managed to win five events. Canada's Anne Heggtveit won the slalom and combined, and America grabbed the silvers—Betsy Snite in the slalom and Penny Pitou, the undisputed star of the Squaw Valley Olympics, in downhill and giant slalom. Another American winner was Ed Scott, whose lightweight, tapered-shaft aluminum ski poles were used by three-fourths of the Olympic racers at Squaw Valley. As impressive as the Americans' results were, the U.S. take-home at Squaw could have been even greater were it not for a broken leg that sidelined Buddy Werner. Tom Corcoran, however, did manage a surprising fourth in giant slalom, the best Olympic finish ever for an American male at the time.

Wallace "Buddy" Werner, of Steamboat Springs, Colorado, was America's hard-luck star, a world-class skier who never won an Olympic medal. Considered, despite his periodic falls, the world's unofficial number one racer, Werner was billed by the press as "the fastest man in the world on skis." Werner won the top European classics: the Holmenkollen-Kandahar downhill (1954, 1956), the Saint Moritz and Zermatt downhills (1956), the Lauberhorn combined (1958), the Kitzbühel downhill (1959)—by 7.3 seconds!—and the Criterium of the First Snow downhill at Val d'Isère, France (1963). He was not only the only American male able to win downhills in his era, he was also one of the world's strongest gate skiers, finishing fourth and fifth in slalom in the 1958 and 1962 World Championships and winning the Holmenkollen-Kandahar giant slalom in 1962.

Buddy Werner was the first of several stars who would bring the United States solidly onto the international ski racing scene. But what the United States had sorely needed for so long, apart from ski racing stars, was organization. And Bob Beattie brought organization to American ski racing.

In the 1950s the United States Ski Team had no full-time staff or coach; in Olympic and World Championship years the U.S. Ski Association traditionally had selected a team and then hired a coach for the season. During that same period a young coach, two years out of Middlebury College in Vermont, where he had coached the ski team with great success, was racking up a reputation for himself as a ski and football coach at Colorado University in Boulder. His name was Bob Beattie, he was twenty-six, and within three years he had brought Colorado University's skiers from nowhere to number one in the country. It was good enough to impress the USSA, which in 1961, as they prepared for the 1962 World Championships, proceeded to offer Beattie a job as the first full-time permanent coach of the U.S. Ski Team. He started with an annual budget of $25,000, which included team expenses *and* his salary.

Beattie drew international attention in 1964 at Innsbruck, Austria, when two of his slalom racers—Billy Kidd and Jimmie Heuga—became the first American male skiers to ever win Olympic gold medals, silver and bronze, respectively. Jean Saubert, on a roll of her own, tied for second in the giant slalom and captured bronze in the slalom. America's Olympic medal count went to four.

As for Buddy Werner, hard luck hit again—he could do no better than eighth in the slalom. However, his encouragement and side-coaching at Innsbruck had inspired Kidd and Heuga to medal-winning performances. Later in the season Werner was killed in an avalanche while making a ski movie with German ski racer Barbi Henneberger at Saint Moritz. Henneberger, who also died in the slide, was being filmed by her fiancé, Willy Bogner, movie producer and heir to the stretch pant fortune.

Ski racing, a heretofore esoteric sport whose heroes were known mostly only to skiers, was finally catching on. The new hero was Frenchman Guy Périllat, who managed the unprecedented feat in the 1961–62 season of winning every major race he entered, something that even Austrian superstar Toni Sailer had not managed to do. But just as it seemed that France's ski racing domination was assured, the Austrians staged a comeback in the 1962 World Championships. The Americans, for their part, finished respectably, with Joan Hannah winning giant slalom bronze and Barbara Ferries capturing downhill bronze.

But the real story was with the Austrians, who managed to bounce back decisively from their 1960 Olympic defeat. Credit Karl Schranz and his fiberglass White Star skis, which rattled the ski racing world.

Fiberglass, as a ski construction material, had first been used in 1954 as a ski base and core-wrapping component by an inveterate tinkerer from Detroit named Danforth Holley. The Holley plastic ski had another feature—a unique L-shaped

Right: *America's Billy Kidd, a "thinking man's skier," was the top U.S. skier of his day. In 1964 he became the first American male to win an Olympic medal. He also put together a strong enough showing at Innsbruck in the downhill and giant slalom to capture the combined.*

Below: *Austria's Toni Sailer, the first (and until Jean-Claude Killy, the only) racer to win three gold medals in a single Winter Olympics (Cortina, 1956), went on to win seven World Championship titles. He parlayed his ski racing success into a film career, business, hotel, a coaching stint with the Austrian team, and directorship of the Kitzbühel ski school.*

Opposite, above: *All of Stowe turned out to welcome Billy Kidd and coach Bob Beattie home after Kidd's 1964 dual-Olympic-medal win. Later the champion moved to Steamboat, Colorado, the unofficial incubator and home of ski Olympians.*

Opposite, below: *Coming up fast on the international race circuit were France's Jean-Claude Killy (left) and Canada's Nancy Greene, two fierce competitors who would dominate skiing in the late sixties.*

Austrians Toni Sailer, Anderl Molterer, and Josl Rieder race in close formation on the head-to-head pro course in Aspen. U.S. pro racing stakes attracted many former ski racing champions to America.

America's Buddy Werner was the best North American skier, and greatest hard-luck athlete, of his era.

edge, which was molded into, rather than screwed on to, the ski. The original patent was later sold to Attenhoffer, a Swiss ski manufacturer; the latter, for the L-shaped edge, was sold to Howard Head, who went on to use it in his famous metal ski. As for Dan Holley, he continued his inventive ways, going on to develop plastic snow, bicycle-chain cleaners, marine accessories, tennis products, and Holley Speed-Wax, still widely used by skiers today.

By 1960 fiberglass was still considered an oddity, a conversation enlivener at ski club gatherings but not much more. Fueling the skepticism over fiberglass was the fact that, by then, there were only two fiberglass skis being made—the Plymold and the Sailer—and neither was particularly outstanding.

By 1961 the number of fiberglass skis had grown to eight out of nearly two hundred skis then being offered, including two from manufacturers who had decided to turn exclusively to fiberglass: the Vuarnet by Rossignol and Kneissl's White Star.

Not only was there resistance to fiberglass at first, there was also a good deal of mystery. Unlike aluminum, a uniform metal, fiberglass was a compound, a cloth of glass fiber strands whose characteristics changed depending upon the amount of epoxy resin that was added to harden it.

Nonetheless, while most of the world was turning to metal skis, Austrian ski maker Franz Kneissl put all his chips on fiberglass. Well, almost all. His Kneissl White Star, which sold for an unprecedented $195 ($100 more than the average racing ski of the time), was really a wood laminate ski with a fiberglass casing. Even so, Kneissl's fiberglass envelope brought new durability—it wouldn't warp when wet—and increased performance. The resiliency of fiberglass meant better shock absorption, increased terrain-hugging ability, and the opportunity for the designer to change the ski's flex pattern more easily than could be done with wood.

Opposite: *France's Guy Périllat was a national hero who in 1961 managed the unprecedented feat of winning every race he entered. He was also one racer who could articulate his team's winning technique. "It is a natural technique," Périllat explained, "based essentially on flexion-extension with or without unweighting of one or two skis and displaying great freedom of spirit, dictated solely by the maintenance of the skier's balance and rejecting everything that seems superfluous or artificial."*

To introduce his new ski Kneissl inveigled Karl Schranz, whom many considered over the hill after his dismal 1960 Olympic performance, to use the White Star. For Kneissl and Schranz it was a marriage made in ski racing heaven. Schranz went on to win the downhill and combined gold in the 1962 World Championships, giving fiberglass new respectability. Within the next ten years, the fiberglass ski chased everything else off the market.

Meanwhile, other events were taking place. A uniform trail-marking system was developed by the National Ski Areas Association. SKI reported that "in 1946 the Aspen Skiing Corporation bought a downtown block from the Denver & Rio Grande for $50. Last season [1963] the half-block next to it sold for $78,000." Sugarbush, Vermont, opened. Marc Bohan of the House of Dior turned his talents to skiwear, proclaiming his designs "the height of elegance for slope and lodge." Oleg Cassini, not to be outdone, put in his two cents, suggesting that "the skier does not have to be sloppy to be rugged and manly." Americans C. B. Vaughan and Dick Dorworth set new world speed records in Portillo, Chile, of more than 106 miles per hour. A charge card for skiers was introduced, permitting skiers to "sign for lodging, meals, drinks, lift tickets, transportation, rentals, and lessons"—cost, six dollars a year. Dave Jacobs was named Canada's first full-time coach. America hosted the first American International Team Races and was promptly pummeled by the Austrians and the French. The Bobby and Teddy Kennedys plus Jackie, Caroline, and John-John spent Christmas skiing in Aspen. Boyne Mountain, Michigan, installed the world's first quadruple chair lift. And the first geländesprung contest was held at Alta, Utah, planting the seed as forerunner of the aerial freestyle meet.

Opinions on just where, and when, freestyle skiing began are mixed. Did it start with Stein Eriksen and his amazing aerial somersaults in the mid-fifties? Or with Doug Pfeiffer and his School for Exotic Skiing? Or did it begin with the diminutive, nearsighted Art Furrer, the Swiss who arrived at New Hampshire's Cannon Mountain in 1962 to teach America acrobatics on skis?

No, freestyle was around long before that. Exhibition skiing, more a free-for-all romp down the hill, was in vogue two hundred years ago in Norway. And the first recorded flip, also performed in Norway, took place in 1907. But there was evidence of early activity in the United States as well. In 1920 *National Geographic* published a picture of Johnny Carleton, a Dartmouth student, doing a flip off a jump during the school's Winter Carnival. The photo, and the story that accompanied it, increased admission requests that season by three hundred percent.

Freestyle skiing as we know it today began in the 1960s. It started with Hermann Goellner, an instructor at Killington, Vermont. He was the first in this country to perform a double flip, then a triple, then a moebius flip—a reverse gainer with a twist. Freestyle continued with the filmed escapades of the Hart Demonstration Team, made up of stunters, flippers, and bumpers like Tom LeRoi, Suzy Chaffee, Roger Staub, Corky Fowler, and Art Furrer.

Ski filmmakers Roger Brown, Barry Corbett, and Dick Barrymore caught the rush and cranked out films that captured the frenzied "freedogger" scene. SKI Magazine profiled Art Furrer in 1964, showed his heel-flicking Franconia Super Dooper Wedeln, rechristened it the Charleston, and introduced acrobatic skiing—an alternative, in freestyle prophet Doug Pfeiffer's words, "to races, where skiers turn only left and right."

While all this was going on, Phil Gerard, a New York choreographer, was experimenting with a Ski Dek in Los Angeles. Among his students were John Clendenin and Johnny Burnett who, together with Gerard, not only developed inventive dance moves on skis but also rigged a diving board, off which they originated such spectacular aerial stunts as the Frog Kick and the Daffy (a midair split with skis).

Early forms of freestyle competition were also in evidence in the sixties. Most notable was Friedl Pfeifer's pro racing tour, which required its racers, as part of their contracts, to perform fancy stunts—often with regrettable results—to whip up enthusiasm for the race events. "We didn't train for it," said Austria's Pepi Gramshammer. "It was just for show. In fact, most of us didn't like it."

Competition or exhibition, freestyle was hatched in defiance of skiing's structured world, as an answer to organized racing, mandated ski school forms, and style-conscious ski techniques. And like the Super Bowl, the hot dog, and Dixieland jazz, it was born, bred, and nurtured in America. Whether America would continue to hold its franchise in the new sport would be determined later.

Another intrinsically American phenomenon of the times was the "megaresort." It had all started in 1955 with Walt Schoenknecht and his master plan for Mount Snow, Vermont. Schoenknecht, who believed that providing on a grand scale for the intermediate skier was the key to a resort's future, was followed six years later by another who felt much the same way—Pete Seibert.

Seibert, raised in Massachusetts, was a Tenth Mountain veteran wounded in the battle of Riva Ridge, a former Aspen ski patroller, international racer, and attender of top French and Swiss resort management schools. He first explored Colorado's Vail valley with pal Earl Eaton, a uranium prospector and native of the area, in 1957. They hiked to the summit of Vail Mountain, whose potential had never been seen because the slopes were out of sight of the highway, saw the mountain's vast bowls and open slopes, and determined that *here* was the ultimate ski resort.

Mill Street in Aspen in the 1950s, with Aspen Mountain (née Ajax) in the background

Opposite: "Doggin' it" fifties style. Today's freestylers have nothing on
skiing's earlier tricksters, particularly
when the fifties skier had to hop-turn
long heavy skis with soft leather boots.

Below: Art Furrer, the fun-loving, nearsighted Swiss, put freestyle on an inno-
vative plane with tricks like the Reuel
(one-legged) Christie. If you had a rea-
sonably decent skating step and could
balance easily on one ski, it was a snap.

Bottom: In the fifties heated outdoor
pools, and their obligatory bathing
beauties, began to compete for the skier's attention.

The resort that Pete built: Vail, Colorado, as it appeared in 1960 (opposite, above), in 1972 (below), and in 1980 (opposite, below). A long way from the rod and gun club that Pete Seibert and Earl Eaton had convinced the valley's landowners the property would be used for, Vail was America's first megaresort with easy skier access to its lifts. The cost to build the resort in 1962 was almost $5 million. By 1971 Vail's expansion had escalated to $20 million. In 1985 the resort was purchased by the Gillett Group for $85 million.

Opposite: *In the East, Stratton Mountain, Vermont, like Vail to the west, also began on a less than grand scale, as one can see in these photographs of the mountain as it looked in 1961 (above) and in 1977 (below). Today eighty-six trails cascade down four hundred acres of groomed terrain on two mountain faces.*

Seibert and Eaton, along with others whose investment dollars they were able to attract, bought up private land in the area under the guise of establishing a rod and gun club and began construction in 1962.

Within seven months, an instant walk-to-the-lifts "Swiss" village called Vail—complete with hotel, motel, stores, homes, apartments, ski trails, and three lifts—was born. Its opening was not auspicious. It had been a miserably dry season in the Rockies, so Seibert hired a band of Ute Indians to dance. Two days later it snowed, and by the end of the first winter the resort had taken its place among the top winter destination spots in the country.

The money it cost to start Vail—almost $5 million—represented nearly the total value of all major American ski areas at the start of World War II. And by 1971 Vail had spent almost $20 million, four times its initial investment, just on expanding the resort.

Resort. That was the key word. And Vail gave new meaning to the term. As I. William Berry wrote in *The Great North American Ski Book*:

> *Where Walt Schoenknecht built a massive, colorful ski area and dreamed of a huge resort interconnected by innovative lift networks, Seibert built that massive, colorful resort at Vail. He conceived the Modern American Ski Town not as a retrofit mining town like Aspen or . . . Breckenridge, not even as a rich man's hideaway (Sun Valley); he conceived it as a place where anyone could be comfortable. . . .*
>
> *How successful was he? In one way or another all the succeeding popular resorts [in Colorado]—Keystone, Copper Mountain, even Steamboat and Snowmass—followed the same basic profile in their early stage of development during the seventies. . . . [But by then,] Vail had already become the queen of American ski resorts.*

The bubble had burst.

Treats for the feet through the ages. Before the introduction of the leather buckle boot (background), an innovation hailed as the greatest breakthrough of its day, ski boots had to be laced (opposite, below), sometimes twice if an inner boot was part of the system. Boots of the day were secured to the ski by a steel cable "bear trap" (opposite, above) that held the heel into the toe plate, and by leather thongs. Curled at the sole and boxy at the toe, the boots were comfortable enough but, being low and soft, weren't much in terms of performance and did little to protect the wearer from ankle twist. The painting below was done by Tenth Mountain artist Jacques Parker for an early cover of SKI Magazine.

Top: *Bob Lange's "plastiques fantastiques," the world's first plastic boot, debuted in 1957.*

Middle: *The 1970 Henke Racer was a high-performance ancestor of Henke's Speedfit, the world's first buckle boot.*

Bottom: *Lange's Competite, the first plastic women's boot, had a decidedly feminine flair.*

Opposite, above: *Scott's lightweight, single-buckle, two-piece ski boot weighed just four and a half pounds a pair, about half the weight of conventional boots of the day.*

Opposite, below: *The Hanson Avanti was the first rear-entry boot. Clean and streamlined, the boot was favored for its comfort (no buckle pressure over the instep) and design.*

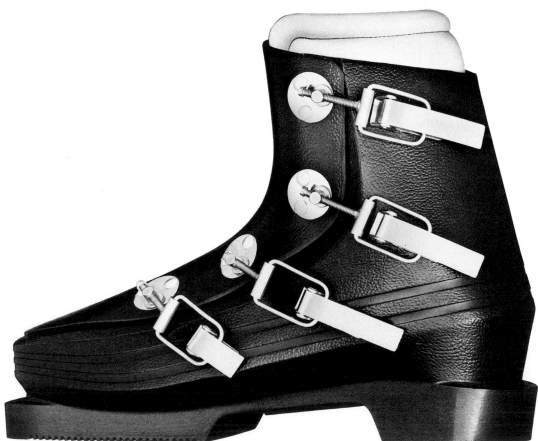

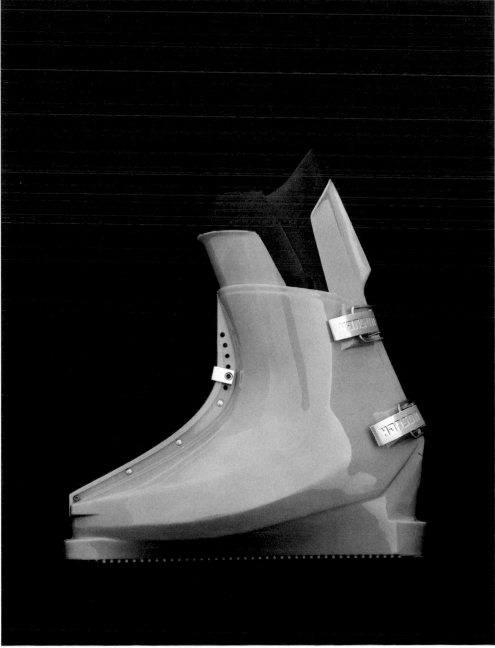

*High tech in the eighties. At the top of
the high-performance category in 1986
were these boots (from left): Raichle's
RX 860, Tecnica's GT for women, the
Nava Sansicario (a soft-sided boot used
with its own binding system), Nordica
NR 990, Koflach CE 500, and the Salomon SX 91E.*

Boot comfort has always been a skier's obsession, and myriad inventions throughout the history of the sport have promised to deliver it. Two that did were the attachable bootwarmer (left), an idea now incorporated in many modern-day boots, and the custom-foamed boot (below). Skiers loved foamed boots—ski shops, which often botched the injection job, didn't.

Opposite: Kneissl's aerodynamic, edge-less, no-buckle, magnetic-retention, fully synthetic skiing system. Designed for "the skier of tomorrow" and shown here in prototype, it never reached the production stage.

Below left: *The simple but reliable Cubco was one of the most popular bindings of its day.*

Below: *The toe-heel unit step-in binding, the most common release system used today, took a giant step toward skier convenience and safety.*

Bottom: *Marker's M4-15 racing binding used a turntable heel that pivoted with the boot in release, reducing sliding friction. Because turntables use a short mounting base, they have minimal effect on ski flex.*

The plate binding, popular in the seventies, fell out of favor with the arrival of advances in plastic bootmaking and binding technology. In the days of leather boot soles, which could become scuffed, warped, and unpredictable in release, metal-to-metal release was determined to be more reliable and, as a result, safer. Below are a few plate bindings of the day (from top): Spademan, Americana, Besser, and Gertsch.

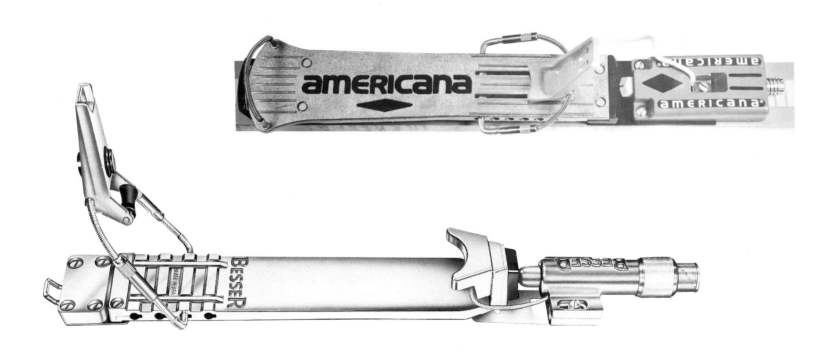

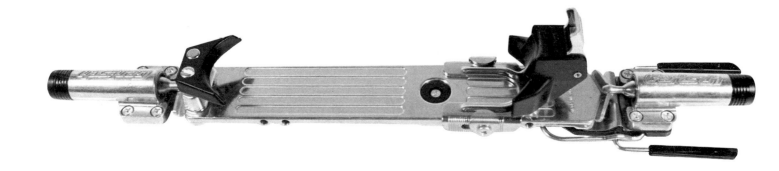

The Look Integral system had the advantage of boot and binding compatibility. The disadvantage was that a ski mounted with an Integral binding couldn't be used with any other boot.

Below: *The revolutionary Burt binding was an adaptation of the plate principle. It featured retractable cables that released the boot from the ski during a fall, then automatically returned the ski to the boot and latched it back into place.*

Bottom: *The ski brake, now a universal feature integrated with the toe unit of modern bindings, was not an immediate success. The fact that it was no longer necessary for ski and skiers to stay attached (a genuine safety factor) caused* some area operators to fear that skiers would drop their skis while riding lifts. With modern, high-elasticity bindings, the concern was soon deemed unwarranted.

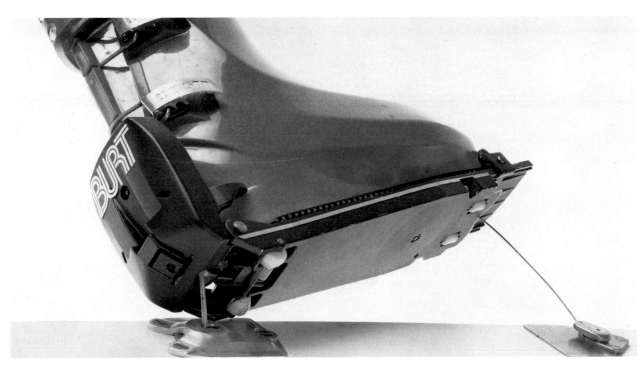

Modern bindings are exclusively of the toe-heel unit variety. All feature antifriction pads at the toe, integrated ski brakes, and hands-off step in/step out convenience. From left: the Tyrolia 490 Diagonal, Salomon 747 Equipe, Geze 952R, and Marker M16

Seen against a background of modern high-performance racing skis and helmets are a group of skis that became "classics" largely because of their success in racing or by a construction breakthrough that radically changed performance or the way we ski. Some classics through the years (bottom left, top to bottom): *the 1935 Eriksen (wide forebody, soft tip and tail), the 1940 Splitkein (laminated construction, used by the Tenth Mountain Division), the 1955 Northland (hickory durability,* shock absorption), *and the 1956 Kästle (soft, limber ash core). (Bottom right, top to bottom: the 1958 Head Standard (durable, flexible metal laminate), the 1962 Kneissl White Star (fiberglass laminate), the 1968 Dynamic VR-17 (wet-wrap fiberglass), and the 1968 Rossignol Strato (gentle-action fiberglass sandwich). These classics, for all their advances, were still a technological giant step behind today's high-performance racing skis.*

Below: *Ski making in the early days required substantial hand labor and hours of finishing work. Howard Head and his metal ski changed all that. Head proved, like Henry Ford, that you could turn out skis, like cars, on a production line.*

Opposite, clockwise from top left: *Over the years, any number of ski construction methods—from wood-core fiberglass sandwich to foam-core wet-wrap torsion box to aluminum honeycomb to omega-shaped metal reinforcement, and other exotic designs—have been attempted.*

Opposite, below: *The Molnar ski, introduced in 1974, used a "prismatic" core, a fiberglass-reinforced plastic prism that allowed the skis' torsional flex to vary according to the skier's needs. Simply put, the ski grew stiffer, providing better edge hold the harder the skier carved a turn.*

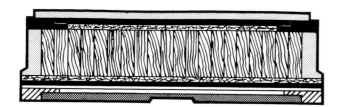

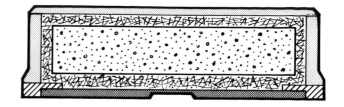

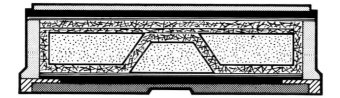

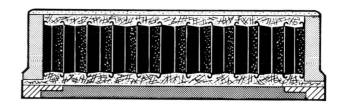

Opposite: *Advances in cross-country, a sport populated in its early days by hide-bound traditionalists, came slower than they did in Alpine. When they did arrive, however, they were just as dramatic. The integrated boot and binding system was one idea that brought new convenience and performance to the sport.*

Cross-country skiing changed forever in the seventies with the arrival of the stepped waxless base. Skiers could now spend more time skiing and less time waxing.

Below: *Ski bases through the ages (bottom to top): wood base with Lignostone edges; plastic base; and three waxless bases—kicker strip, fishscale, and inlaid mohair strips*

Bottom: *The waxing procedure, now outmoded*

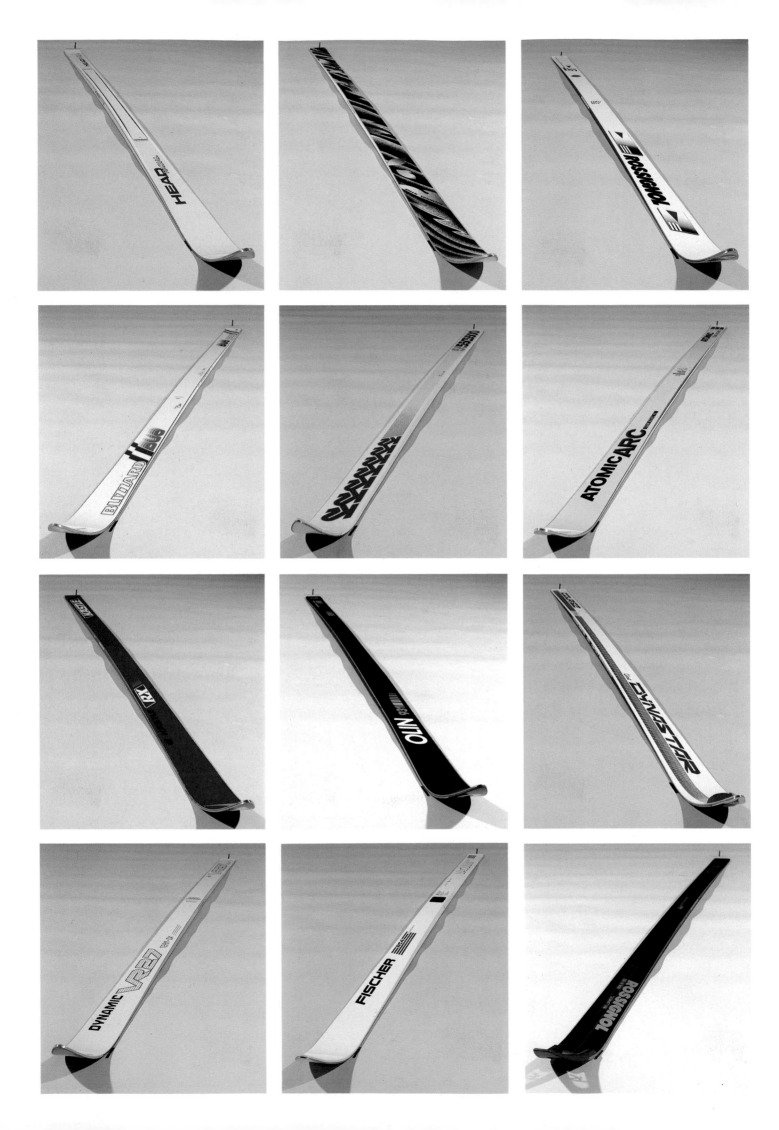

Opposite: *Several popular brands and models of modern-day skis. Cosmetics can change but the shape lingers on. From the top, left to right: Head Radial Graphite, Kneissl Avant Garde Star, Rossignol 3G Kevlar, Blizzard Duo 2000, K2 5500, Atomic RS, Kästle Equipe S, Olin 931, Dynastar Course GS, Dynamic VR-27, Fischer RC4, and Rossignol Quantum*

Fun for the future? Though skiing purists could accept, however reluctantly, the arrival of the monoski (left), the spectacle of a snowboard (below), requiring more the skills of a surfer or skateboarder than those of a skier, was more than most could handle. Two advantages of both: no poles were needed and your tips never crossed.

PART IV
ANYTHING GOES

If there was a period in American skiing in which the saying "anything goes" applied, it was the era 1966–75. It was a time of equipment experimentation, of changes in technique, of freedom and expression in skiing.

SKI Magazine published its first ski nude, screened discreetly by a tree, to a storm of protest; the sexual revolution had not yet arrived. The magazine followed, somewhat more conservatively, with its "Ski Bird" series, clothed foldout pinups of "the finest feathers on the slopes." This also bombed. Psychedelic warmup pants in Mellow Yellow, Crazy Orange, and Lolita Pink took off as the latest in ski fashion. Japan's Yuichiro Miura, equipped with a parachute as brake, schussed the South Col of Mount Everest. Sylvain Saudan skied the West Face of the Eiger. The rush to "first descents" had begun.

If one-upmanship was the rule of the day, it wasn't lost on the equipment designers, who introduced some of the strangest contrivances yet.

The Rosemount boot, for one. Billed as a "ski boot born of intensive study, modern methods, and exceptional engineering design," the Rosemount was a plastic boot with foot entry at the side. It displayed a variety of unusual features. To achieve a custom fit, the boot came with special fitting "pillows." The problem was that once your feet felt snug, it was impossible to close the boot. A unique closure system—a canvaslike flap that stretched across the front of the boot and fastened with two buckles—was supposed to secure the boot. It proved more adept at keeping the wearer in a state of semifrostbite. The Rosemount proved particularly unnerving to ski instructors, who found that it suddenly became detached during class demonstrations.

The era produced other lemons. The Lange Competition, a one-piece boot, was so stiff that it led to shin injuries commonly called Lange Bangs and earned the boot the nickname "stovepipe." What's more, it didn't close properly because the shell flaps butted up against each other. Scott, a Sun Valley firm that had made its name in ski poles, also missed with its introduction of an ABS plastic boot touted as lighter and stronger than any boot yet made. It was strong enough, but the ABS material was also very brittle, causing the boot to shatter in any temperature below freezing. Some skiers were known to go through as many as seven pairs a season, each one under a new warranty, until even the ski shops gave up. Scott abandoned bootmaking in 1979.

Another innovation that was soon abandoned was boot foaming. Foaming was a custom-fitting process in which the skier's foot, through an injection of polyurethane foam into an inner boot, was virtually cooked in place. In 1970 it was the rage—a hit with everyone except the ski shops, which found the process complex, messy, and costly, as a boot foamed improperly had to be thrown away. Two years later boot foaming was history.

The era also produced other dubious achievements. The principle of the Marker FD Rotamat binding was sensible enough—a spring release system at the heel set on a pedestal that rotated as the skier's heel moved, preventing unwanted

Yuichiro Miura—ski racer, speed skier, and Japanese legend—on Mount Everest before his historic plunge. Miura's feat required eight hundred high-altitude porters, twenty-seven tons of luggage, sixty-five-pound packs, oxygen, a parachute, and pure grit. Hitting a speed of more than 100 miles per hour just six seconds from the top, Miura skied 6,600 feet in two minutes, twenty seconds—then fell 1,320 feet, losing both skis, and stopping just 250 feet short of a gaping crevasse. Said Miura during his Everest ascent, "I have climbed many summits but this is different. Something has happened to me. For the first time, I am afraid." The film of Miura's feat, The Man Who Skied Everest, won an Academy Award.

Cross-country was discovered by American skiers in a big way in the seventies. Serenity, a slower pace, kinship with nature, and escape from skiing's crowds were the draws. The cross-country skier below tours the snowfields of Mount Rose, Nevada.

Below: *Did we say cross-country was
an escape from skiing's crowds? Some
will bring competition, and crowds, to
anything they do. Here, eastern skiers
bound off in a George Washington's
Birthday race. Virtually any holiday is
reason enough to stage a cross-country
race.*

Bottom: *Cross-country workshop at
Dartmouth College in Hanover, New
Hampshire*

premature release. But if racers favored the Rotamat for its retention, recreational skiers cursed its complexity. When the heel released, its spring assembly would split into several pieces, inspiring some users, forced to reassemble the unit with gloves on in deep snow, to call it the Explodamat.

Whatever the Rotamat's quirks, it was an engineering marvel compared to the Americana. A plate binding, the Americana had steel surfaces that would rust—and then stick together. As a result, the binding tended not to release at all, even when banged with a hammer.

Skis also came in for an occasional experimental blunder. Howard Head's first fiberglass ski, the Killy, named after and promoted by Jean-Claude Killy, the 1968 triple-gold Olympic champion, had the unfortunate tendency to peel apart after a brisk run through the moguls. The problem at the time was that no one knew much about laminating fiberglass. The ski also had cosmetic shortcomings; maroon in color, it turned bright pink in the sunlight, leading some owners to claim that it probably had a bad conscience.

If the decade produced some misfits, the era also saw some genuine equipment breakthroughs—the ski brake, for one. Today used in virtually all binding systems, it was greeted with mild skepticism when Mitch Cubberley introduced it in the late sixties. A slender, spring-loaded steel paddle, the "Ski Stopper," as Cubberley called his brake, grabbed the snow to stop the ski's descent if it was unhinged by a releasing boot. The concept took a few years to catch on, but when it did,

Opposite: *Jean-Claude Killy, on his way to the first of his three Olympic medals in the 1968 Winter Games at Grenoble, France. Killy had little regard for the "posed" racing techniques of his day, going all out instead with his "brink of disaster" technique—characterized by a sitting back, skiing on his uphill ski, and falling, always falling. "If only he would use sound technique," said one expert, "he'd be fantastic."*

Left: *Killy in 1973 in action on the U.S. pro circuit*

longthongs and safety straps beat a hasty retreat. And with them went the scars and bruises that skiers wore from released, but still tenuously attached, windmilling skis.

It was also the era of Dr. Richard Spademan's amazing "toeless wonder"—a plate binding that released the boot from the sides rather than at the toe and heel.

Even cross-country skiing, long thought the province of the skiing purist and backcountry loner, became the focus of new technology with the introduction of the waxless ski. What caused all the excitement was the "fishscale" base. Originally conceived by inventor William Bennett as a way to make Alpine skis slide faster, the base, which could both grip *and* slide, found a future instead on cross-country skis manufactured by Trak. Out went the waxing mystique, in came millions of skiers attracted by the new effortlessness of the sport. By 1973 one out of every four pairs of skis purchased were cross-country skis.

Meanwhile, other things were happening. President Gerald Ford vacationed at Vail, Colorado. The press, gathered in a "bumble watch," saw him obligingly walk into a moving chair lift. Adding insult to injury, it was revealed to an astonished public that America's first skiing president was not Jerry Ford, not Cal Coolidge, but Teddy Roosevelt. The K2 Ski Company introduced its bubble gum cards—sepia photo profiles of K2 factory workers in nineteenth-century dress—and quickly became known as skiing's "fun bunch." Magic Mountain, Vermont, became the first resort to limit lift ticket sales—the numbers of skiers were growing faster than the lifts. Squaw Valley, California, installed the world's fastest tram. Novelist Oakley Hall wrote *The Downhill Racers*. Though it wasn't a best-seller, actor Robert Redford took an option on the book, produced the movie *Downhill Racer,* and the story became a cult hit. Loon Mountain and Waterville Valley opened in New Hampshire. The Sierra Club squashed development of Mineral King, a proposed $50 million, four-season resort to be built by the Disney Corporation. American Steve McKinney broke the world speed record at Cervinia, Italy, clocking 117.663 miles per hour. Killington and a dozen other resorts in the East opened at Thanksgiving as a regular practice, giving easterners another much-wanted four weeks of skiing. The war between the developers and the ecologists escalated in Vermont and the Rockies. Skitronic was introduced as the newest ski teaching aid. A device mounted on the front of the boot, it went "beep" whenever the skier failed to lean forward to properly pressure his ski tips in the turn. Snowbird opened as Utah's first ultramodern destination ski resort, followed by Park City, Solitude, Powder Mountain, Nordic Valley, and Robert Redford's Sundance. Roger Brown and Barry Corbett teamed to produce *Ski the Outer Limits,* a cinematic tour de force that went on to outsell every ski film in history. Chet Huntley left television to start Big Sky, Montana. By 1975 the skier population had reached an estimated five million.

In 1966 the FIS Alpine World Championships were held in Portillo, Chile, the first time ever in the southern hemisphere. The Austrian team seemed old and tired. The Americans could win only one medal, a bronze in slalom by Penny McCoy. France's Jean-Claude Killy, showing the skill and daring that would later earn him world acclaim, won the downhill. Ski theoretician Georges Joubert wrote of Killy's "reckless and radical technique," describing Killy's use of the step turn plus his "serpent" technique, as Joubert then called anticipation, a technique of leading the turn with the upper body and letting the lower body follow. Joubert was the first to recognize the beginnings of avalement, using down unweighting and extension in conjunction with a step turn.

Opposite: *Killy relaxes before a World Cup race. The French ace was as adept at pranks as he was at winning ski races. He doffed his pants in midair during a jumping exhibition, drove a Volkswagen into the lobby of a hotel, and was known for his deadly aim with seltzer bottles. But it was his reckless, win-at-all-costs technique that earned him victories on the mountain. Said Killy, "Every race is a bet with myself."*

Below: *Killy in slalom action at Vail, Colorado. Killy's "serpent" technique was characterized by an elasticity of motion, the skis virtually flat, with minimal edging, making for a lighter, freer ski. "It is simply the end product of all that's been tried by my generation," said Killy modestly. "There will be other ways."*

An American album of period players: Willy "It's Vun to Vin!" Schaeffler (right) parlayed a brilliant coaching record at Denver University (13 of 18 national championships, 100 wins in 123 ski meets) into a berth as U.S. Ski Team Alpine Director in 1970–73. His 1972 U.S. Olympic team won gold and bronze at Sapporo. American ski racing stars of the period included (clockwise from below): Kiki Cutter, the first American to win a World Cup race (1968); Marilyn Cochran, winner of the 1969 World Cup in giant slalom and eldest of Vermont's famous ski racing family; Tyler Palmer, unpredictable, rebellious, an American "best hope" for a medal at Sapporo in 1972 who could do no better than a ninth; Spider Sabich, plagued by injuries (he broke his legs seven times in eight years with the U.S. Ski Team), never won a World Cup race (but was second twice), and could muster only a fifth at the Sapporo Winter Olympics.

Previous page and below: *World Cup racers have always enjoyed the tour's spring swing to North America. And one of their favorite stops—its Alpine charm reminds them of home—is Vail, Colorado. Among North Americans competing in the early World Cup were* (bottom, left to right) *America's Rick Chaffee, Dennis McCoy, and Canada's Nancy Greene.*

In 1967 SKI's European editor Serge Lange founded the concept of a World Cup of Alpine Skiing, a season-long series of races to recognize the world's best skiers. The magazine took a further step by announcing its Nations Cup, awarded to the country whose individual racers amass the greatest number of World Cup points. The first World Cup was won, as was the second in 1968, by Killy and by Canada's Nancy Greene, with France taking the Nations Cup both years. Killy, as impressive in his après-ski pursuits as he was on the course, left a memorable mark on Jackson Hole, Wyoming, site of the first World Cup finals. John Fry, in SKI, reported his impressions:

> The origin of the term après-ski is unknown. It strikes me as a very sophisticated and dainty expression dreamed up by an interior decorator in Mégève, France. . . . But the blowout at Jackson Hole was, by any account, the triple-gold-medal winner of all time in après-ski. Austrians embraced French embraced Swiss embraced Americans. In one friendly gesture, someone hit Austria's Karl Schranz over the head with a bottle. Schranz blinked his eyes a couple of times and eventually resumed talking to the lady next to him.
>
> The banquet that followed was what you might expect if you put two hundred intoxicated bakers in a room together. Buns flew from table to table. German and French songs resounded. Someone tried to make a speech. Eventually, they passed out the trophies. A couple of racers had to be bodily assisted to the platform to receive their awards. Somewhere along the way, Killy offended a bouncer. He went chasing the World Cup champion, but Marielle Goitschel, Killy's teammate, stuck out her foot and tripped him. It was later reported that the bouncer had broken his clavicle.

As remarkable as were the World Cup performances of Killy and Greene, so were the skis on which they rode to victory—Killy on his Dynamic VR-17s, Greene on her Rossignol Stratos. The VR-17, developed in 1962 by French furniture maker Paul Michal, would go on to become a classic among racing skis. Like Austria's Franz Kneissl, Michal saw fiberglass as the future for skis. But Michal didn't apply the fiberglass in sheets as had Kneissl. Instead, he impregnated the fiberglass with resin and wrapped it while wet around a core in strips, like the encasement of a mummy. The process, called wet-wrap, gave a ski designer greater control over a ski's torsional (twisting) flex. As the avalement, or "sit-back," technique developed, so did the VR-17—to become the first soft-tip, stiff-tail, modern high-performance ski. The VR-17 not only had a unique flex pattern, its sidecut was back waisted as well. With the narrowest part of the ski under the heel instead of the instep, the skier could make the VR-17 do truly marvelous things: carve, by leaning forward, or accelerate out of the turn, by leaning back. It was on the VR-17 that Killy won his historic three gold medals at the Winter Olympics in 1968.

At about the same time that Dynamic's Michal was building the first VR-17, Rossignol, another French ski manufacturer, was also experimenting with fiberglass. The result was the Strato, which, though it featured the same soft-tip, stiff-tail performance as the VR-17, was somewhat gentler than Dynamic's fiberglass tube. It became, under Nancy Greene, the premier women's racing ski. It also caught on in a big way with recreational skiers who, beginner or expert, found its precise but gentle performance much to their liking.

The French, in fact, had by the late 1960s put a lock on ski technique, theory, racing, and equipment. They had also produced ski racing's first millionaire, Jean-Claude Killy, who signed on with American sports-star builder Mark McCormack for a multitude of rich endorsement contracts.

The French, although they didn't know it at the time, also had made an impact on recreational ski racing in America. In 1968 SKI Magazine editor John Fry, impressed with the Chamoix series of citizen races held throughout the French Alps, thought about instituting a similar program for skiers in the United States. The result was SKI's National Standard Race, or NASTAR, consisting of a national handicapping system in which the entrant could win medals merely by improving his time at his own speed. Jimmie Heuga, 1964 Olympic bronze medalist, became the first NASTAR pacesetter, establishing a zero handicap against which weekend skiers tried to match themselves. It was the closest thing to par in golf. Former U.S. Ski Team czar Bob Beattie became NASTAR national commissioner in 1969 and within two decades would expand NASTAR to more than one hundred fifty resorts in thirty states, making it the largest ski racing program in the world.

Beattie would also take yet another form of ski competition—pro racing—from almost complete obscurity to network television. In the early sixties the International Professional Ski Racers Association had formed to organize a series of money races. The competitors consisted of a group of ex-racers, mostly Europeans, and the events were run on head-to-head parallel courses. The pros, at their best, organized ten races and brought in $100,000 in prize money. Then the circuit went broke.

Enter Beattie in 1970, and suddenly pro racing was a new ball game. He built the season purse to $800,000, added big-name sponsors, and convinced ABC-TV, for which he had been working as a sports commentator, to add pro ski racing to its schedule. Presto—the American public had now been suitably introduced to ski racing, and its television helpings grew as Beattie, an influential voice in international racing circles, campaigned vigorously to bring World Cup ski racing, traditionally a European-dominated competition waged throughout the Alps, to America.

In other developments of the era, Austrian world champion Erika Schinegger underwent a sex change, became Erik, raced against the men, and married. The National Environmental Policy Act was passed, banning all new resort building on U.S.

Opposite: *NASTAR allows the recreational skier to compete not only against himself through handicap improvement but against the nation's top pro pacesetter and all NASTAR skiers across the country.*

Below: *Women's pro racing, a season-long series of head-to-head races pitting former World Cup and Olympic skiers, began in the seventies with a $40,000 three-event purse. Within four years, the tour had grown to ten events and $165,000 in prize money.*

Forest Service land in the Rockies and the Sierra Nevada, and Vermont enacted a law cracking down even more severely on ski resort development. One hundred lift operators, ticket takers, bus drivers, and ski patrollers from Vail went to "smile school." Squaw Valley skier-adventurer Rick Sylvester skied off the top of Yosemite's El Capitan and parachuted to the valley floor—twice. Denver was selected as the site for the 1976 Winter Olympics, but ecology-conscious voters in a state-financing referendum stonewalled the Games with the bumper-sticker campaign "Don't Californicate Colorado." Ski length, under the influence of freestyle and GLM, dropped another couple of inches; the bottom dropped out of the market for long skis. Sweden's Ingemar Stenmark became the first racer outside the Alps to win the World Cup. Jet Stix, portable spoilers for attaching to the rear of ski boots, were introduced to help skiers sit back on the tails of their skis. It was, according to theoreticians of the day, "a gross misinterpretation of the French technique." Inner Skiing, a new "soar like an eagle, pounce like a tiger" method of learning through analytical/physical hemispheric isolation of the brain, was introduced by sports guru Tim Gallwey. Most instructors labeled it "flaky" and decided to stay with more conventional, skills-oriented teaching techniques.

Meanwhile, Americans were running up some impressive results in international racing. Billy Kidd, after eight grueling years on the world racing circuit, his ankles taped and his sore back corseted, became the first North American male to win a gold medal in the World Championships. He did it in 1970 in the combined at Val Gardena, Italy, with a slalom run the equal of his Olympic silver-medal performance in 1964 and the best downhill run by an American in eighteen years. The next day he announced that he was turning pro. Two years later, in 1972 at Sapporo, Japan, America's Barbara Ann Cochran, skiing all out in the slalom, captured the first Olympic gold medal for the United States since Andrea Mead's two-medal wins twenty years earlier. The Swiss, Italians, and the first Spaniard ever to take a medal—Francisco Fernandez-Ochoa—shut out the Austrians and the French men but for a single bronze. It was also a first for Masayoshi Veda, who devised the first drug tests for Olympic ski racers. "It is difficult," she observed, "to create an atmosphere conducive to

Austria's irascible Karl Schranz, ever ski racing's black sheep, skied begrudgingly in Jean-Claude Killy's shadow in the sixties. Combative and tenacious, Schranz was considered washed up after a mediocre 1968 season, then came back to win the 1979 and 1980 World Cups. One of the sport's most durable competitors, Schranz was a fearless downhiller whose ski racing career spanned twenty-nine years. Schranz won virtually every honor that skiing could bestow—except the coveted, and illusive, Olympic gold medal.

urination.'' Before the Games even began, Avery Brundage, the crusty chairman of the International Olympic Committee, banned Austria's Karl Schranz for ''professionalism.'' Brundage's act was to make Schranz a national hero back home. (If all else failed, Schranz could have returned to recording. His first record, called ''Toi Toi Toi,'' was a modest success in Austria. Former ski racing greats Toni Sailer and Guy Périllat, who also tried their hand at recording, flopped.)

But the real interest in skiing in America wasn't with Olympic racing, World Championship competition, World Cup events, or the pros. During the period 1966–75 America had a love affair with freestyle.

The first National Championships of Exhibition Skiing, held at Waterville Valley, New Hampshire, were the brainchild of Doug Pfeiffer, founder of the School of Exotic Skiing, and Tom Corcoran, former American Olympic ski racer and owner of Waterville Valley. It was a one-run-per-contestant event held on Waterville's True Grit trail. Chevrolet, the first big

Canada's Nancy Greene—fiery, spirited, pugnacious—earned a victory record matched by few others. She won the first overall World Cup in 1967, winning seven of seventeen races, then repeated by winning the cup again in 1968 after capturing gold and silver at the Grenoble Winter Olympics.

Jean-Claude Killy, the other half of the 1967 winning World Cup team, bullets downs the giant slalom course during the end-of-year finals at Jackson Hole, Wyoming. The season, the first for the World Cup, was only a prelude to Killy's 1968 triple-Olympic-gold-medal win.

Jet Stix, plastic spoilers that could be at-tached to the rear of ski boots, were an affordable alternative to newer highback boots. The purpose of both was to help skiers achieve a "sit-back" position.

sponsor of freestyle, put up cash and a Stingray as prizes. Appearance money was also thrown in to tempt the best western skiers east. And the lexicon of stunts was growing: Mule Kicks, Backscratchers, Upsprungs, Tip Rolls, Wheelies, Shoulder Rolls, Spread Eagles, Layouts, Helicopters, Polish Doughnuts, and Worm Turns. SKI's Peter Miller reported on the event:

> *They came from the West, and from out of the woodwork and out of the woods. . . . The event turned out to be everything Pfeiffer said free skiing could be. It was exciting, even in the miserable weather that pre-vailed. Little Bob Bennet from Sun Valley, wearing a gigantic hat, sailed into the woods and, everybody assumed, disaster—then flashed out seventy yards below, hit a bump, and jumped back to midtrail. Bob Burns did tremendous wheelies. Hermann Goellner flipped and won the Stingray. Suzy Chaffee, resplen-dent in red, black, and white ski tights, did a ballet performance. She wore short skis, which no one liked, and was the only woman to compete. She was great to look at.*
>
> *Wayne Wong had hitchhiked from Vancouver to compete. His mogul skiing wasn't very good and neither were his aerials, but his ballet was something else. Wong did Windmill Crossovers, 360s, Tip Rolls, Helicopters, and his special, the Wong Banger. How could you go wrong with an impish smile, a Charlie Chan name, and a Wong Banger?*

How did it feel to be a freestyle skier in the early years? Said Jake Jakespeare, "We gave no thought to safety. It wasn't even a factor. People who were concerned with safety just didn't get involved in the sport—let them go ski the hill. This was a daredevil sport. Those of us who first flipped developed a special bond with each other. We had to take risks."

Freestyle—its stars, its language, its lifestyle—took the ski world by storm in the early seventies. By 1975 competitors had organized and hired their own agents, the circuit had attracted big-name sponsors like Chevrolet, Midas, Budweiser, and Colgate, and total prize money for the season had jumped to $550,000.

How much could a professional freestyler make? Up to $40,000 a year with sponsorships, promotional appearances, and prize money.

How did a freestyler feel about his sport? Scott Brooksbank: "It's an attitude—of harmony, of living, of environment. You're breaking away. It's rebellious desire. You're rebelling against skiing on the ground."

Mike Lund: "You get ripped away from controls, from society, from taxes, from cutting your hair."

John Clendenin: "In freestyle you can feel moments when it happens, when you know God is on your side."

Bob Salerno: "I love to get upside down. I'm real loose in the air."

Eddie Ferguson: "The trip is the limit and it gets broken every day."

How did nonfreestylers feel about freestyle?

"My daughter will never marry a freestyler. Good blood and bad blood don't mix," a French father warned an American hotdogger who fell in love with his daughter.

"It's dissolute. It makes me sick," said Al Raine, former Alpine program director of the Canadian Ski Team.

"Hotdoggers are frustrated racers," said Mickey Cochran, former head coach of the U.S. Ski Team.

"It blows the mind and screws up the hill," said Robert Redford, actor and ski area operator.

Then there were those who saw freestyle as a move to return the ski sport to its origins. New York movie critic and ardent skier Archer Winsten was one. "Is skiing a risk sport," he asked, "or is it croquet? When skiing is dehorned to the level of a social function, a high fashion show, a nightly round of romance where no one gets hurt unless a girl's feelings are abraded, when the risk is reduced, then the real and unique values of skiing become debased. The pressure's off. Skiing moves over among the sports that make no demand and exact no penalties."

Freestyle created its own look. To be considered a real free dogger of the day required that you: let your hair grow long; plug into a set of Astraltunes (precursor of the Walkman); wear love beads or a peace pendant; adopt a western look, complete with cowboy hat, shirt, hair, and moustache; wear Captain America or appliquéd pants ("Do your own thing" was rapidly coming to skiwear.); tie a bandana to your leg; and own a pair of banana boots, which touched off the seventies color explosion in equipment.

Whatever a skier's clothing preference, skiwear designers were turning out individualized styles that were guaranteed to make your ski wardrobe the first of its kind on the block. A real skier was judged not only by his clothing but by the number of bags he owned to haul his gear and clothing around. Mused SKI travel editor Abby Rand, "To lug all this stuff

Skiing came flipping, twisting, and kicking its way to notoriety in the seventies with the introduction of freestyle. It was then called "hotdogging," and one of its earliest practitioners was former U.S. Olympic skier Suzy Chaffee, here strutting her stuff in the bumps in an exhibition at Sun Valley.

Most spectacular of freestyle's disciplines was, and is, the aerial event. Mike Grazier and Roger Evans (below) uncork a hand-held back flip at Vail, Colorado.

Below left: *Aerial freestyle, if nothing else, presented the skier with a new way of looking at the sport.*

Below right: *Real hotdoggers, like this youngster at Killington, Vermont, had little use for fancy built jumps—bona-fide space invaders used available terrain to spring for air.*

around, you need a great big suitcase. Your boots won't fit in it, so you need a boot carrier. You need a boot carrier bag to put the carrier in. You need a ski bag to put your skis in, a pole bag to put your poles in, and another bag to put all the bags in while you ski.''

Meanwhile, freestyle experienced growing pains. With the promise of big dollars came fragmentation within the ranks. A group of top stunters, the hot twenty-five freestylers of 1973–74, split off from the International Freestyle Skiers Association—formed the previous season to set safety and competitor-certification standards—to establish their own organization, Professional Freestyle Associates, and began negotiating with sponsors to hold their own meets. The competitions were to be limited to twenty-five ''selected participants'' (presumably themselves), and one of the incentives PFA offered

Freestyle, with its counterculture look, lifestyle, and derring-do, became the rage throughout ski country. Even California skiers, such as this one at Heavenly Valley (opposite), known for their conservatism, mild manneredness, and disdain for the unusual, were known to pop an occasional flip.

sponsors was the exhibition of double back flips, aerial stunts that were banned under IFSA rules. The power grab backfired, egos clashed, legal wrangles ensued, sponsor money dried up, professional hotdogging took a bath, and freestyle suddenly found itself drowning in bad ink. Its credibility in doubt, the sport withdrew to lick its wounds, ponder its future, and reorganize as an amateur competition that, ten years later, would finally regain the respect and support of the ski establishment.

However divisive freestyle became as a sport in the seventies, its influence continued to be evident in ski design. Differing sharply from recreational skis, freestyle skis were wider, shorter, often with turned up tails and grooveless bottoms. Ski length, under the influence of both freestyle and GLM, dropped another couple of inches. SKI called it "The Shorting of America" and observed that "at the big Aspen ski swap in November, more than five hundred pairs of skis two hundred centimeters or longer were put up for sale. Four pairs were bought."

This was not to say that all skiers favored short skis. Traditional-length skiers bellowed, "Short skis make minefields out of mogul fields," accused "midget skis" of creating "staircase bumps and nasty snow conditions," and countered with a bumper-sticker campaign to "Stamp Out the Short Ski Menace."

Although isolationism wasn't exactly a general trend in the early seventies, evidence of it was suddenly surfacing in skiing. There was, first, a proposal put forth by officials of the U.S. Ski Association in 1967 that foreign competitors be excluded from U.S. national ski jumping championships, the fear being that American jumpers were becoming "horribly demoralized by the overwhelming victories of Norwegian and Finnish jumpers." SKI, of another opinion, called the resolution "silly" and editorialized: "Foreign jumpers are just the sort of high-caliber competition our boys need if they are to emulate the world's best." The proposal, after considerable debate, was voted down.

While the USSA came to its collective senses, the U.S. State Department, in its campaign to hold the alien population in check, was determined to hold its ground. Observed SKI:

The gray mist of federal bureaucracy, which until now has hovered lightly at the edges of the ski world, now threatens to spread itself liberally about in the otherwise sunny world we all love. It all started when Washington decided that the ski instructor is not, as heretofore, a specialized and desirable personage in terms of our national economy. No, says the State Department's Naturalization and Immunization Service, it is rather the case that the ski instructor from abroad, along with Mexican wetbacks and Canadian apple pickers, is competing for scarce American jobs.

While some skiers were exploring the limits of freestyle in the seventies, others—like these skier-campers on Fresh Field Glacier in Alberta, Canada—just went exploring.

Canada, on the other hand, was worrying about its brain drain—the exodus of talented Canadians to better-paying positions in the United States. The reverse, however, was true in skiing. Scores of would-be American instructors were flocking to Canada to get their basic training, much to the consternation of the Canadian ski establishment.

Differences over theory in ski technique were becoming every bit as spirited as instructor controversies over how skiing skills should properly be taught. One of the simplest answers to the whole issue of instruction and technique was given by Chicago osteopathic surgeon Dr. William J. Mauer, who ventured, "If you've been taking lessons for years and still can't ski parallel, you probably have a short leg."

Professor Stefan Kruckenhauser of Saint Anton, Austria, acknowledged guru of international ski technique, was of another mind. For years, skiers had been taught to up-unweight, or hop a bit, to get their skis to start a turn. In 1971 Kruckenhauser and the Austrian demonstration team showed another way, previously reserved only for expert skiers. It was called down-unweighting and it opened up yet another option for the struggling intermediate. Short skis, still considered a mixed blessing by many instructors, were given Professor Kruckenhauser's official approval. At the 1971 Interski, the Austrians, the French, the Americans, the Swiss, and the Germans all included GLM demonstrations as part of their presentations. Said Kruckenhauser, "An instructor today who starts a pupil on normal-length skis is a gangster."

The University of Utah, meanwhile, pioneered with the first study that answered the burning question of how women *really* rate male ski instructors. The surprise conclusion was that women were not only less happy with, but also more demanding of their ski instructors than men. The women's responses showed a particularly high degree of dissatisfaction with the amount of standing around during a class lesson; compared to the men, women were towers of impatience. Women, the study further revealed, wanted more individual attention. The women also felt that ski lessons were given in far too rigid and tense an atmosphere. Finally, the women felt, more so than the men, that ski instructors should be much more competent than they appeared to be.

If most skiers were still trying to master parallel technique, others were taking the sport to new heights. Fritz Stammberger skied down the 14,300-foot face of North Maroon Bell in Aspen and claimed he had an easy time of it, falling only once— over a 15-foot cliff. Bill Briggs, ski school director at Storm King, Wyoming, skied down the Grand Teton near Jackson Hole, a feat previously thought impossible, and also fell off a cliff. He did Stammberger one better by triggering an avalanche on his way down. Surfer Mike Doyle proclaimed that "skis weren't made for skiing" and set about building a single ski that was fine for surfers but required substantially more skill from skiers than normally required for skiing. Jeff Jobe showed the world how to hang glide on skis, stating proudly, "We all fly—except my mother." And Mount Snow's Rudi Wyrsch schussed, with the help of arresting ropes, the facade of the Sheraton Hotel in Boston.

Given America's early preoccupation with the more serious side of skiing, these events came as a refreshing change. Observed SKI in 1968 in "A Case of Overkill": "Present-day ski instruction is creating a whole generation of skiing robots. The remedy? Put plain, old-fashioned fun back into learning how to ski." Editor John Fry, echoing SKI's campaign three years later, wrote, "It is one of the remarkable curiosities of our age that we have managed to make our recreational amusements into serious endeavors. Thus, for many people, skiing has become not so much a joyful occasion of play in the snow, but more a deadly concern with technique, with equipment, with clothing, lodging, lifts, and the biomechanics

Below: *Torchlight parades like this one in Banff, Alberta, were de rigueur in the sixties. For special-event, race-day, or ceremonial openers, torch-wielding skiers, snaking like a glowing serpent down the mountain, never failed to impress.*

Opposite: *Alberta delivers skiing variety aplenty—whether powder, steeps, cruising runs, cross-country trails, or as here, bumps—plus some of the most spectacular mountain scenery a skier will ever see.*

of skiing. . . . [This] obscene concern with the technology of skiing is destroying the spirit of a sport whose essence is the beauty and exhilaration of the outdoors.''

Among those skiers who did not take the sport particularly seriously were the celebrities—film stars, politicians, sports heroes, recording stars, and other public idols who streamed to the early celebrity ski events, made-for-media happenings that would soon become a ski season fixture.

Actor Hugh O'Brian, skiing in a celebrity event for the first time, asked, "What do I play—a slalom pole?" SKI, in reporting on a race at Bear Valley, California, followed the practice runs of film star Lloyd Bridges: "In the course of a single day, Bridges managed to break one ski, put both bindings out of commission, and lose his glasses, all in separate accidents. He then capped the day by running into Beau Bridges, his son, who was lying on the snow after taking a fall."

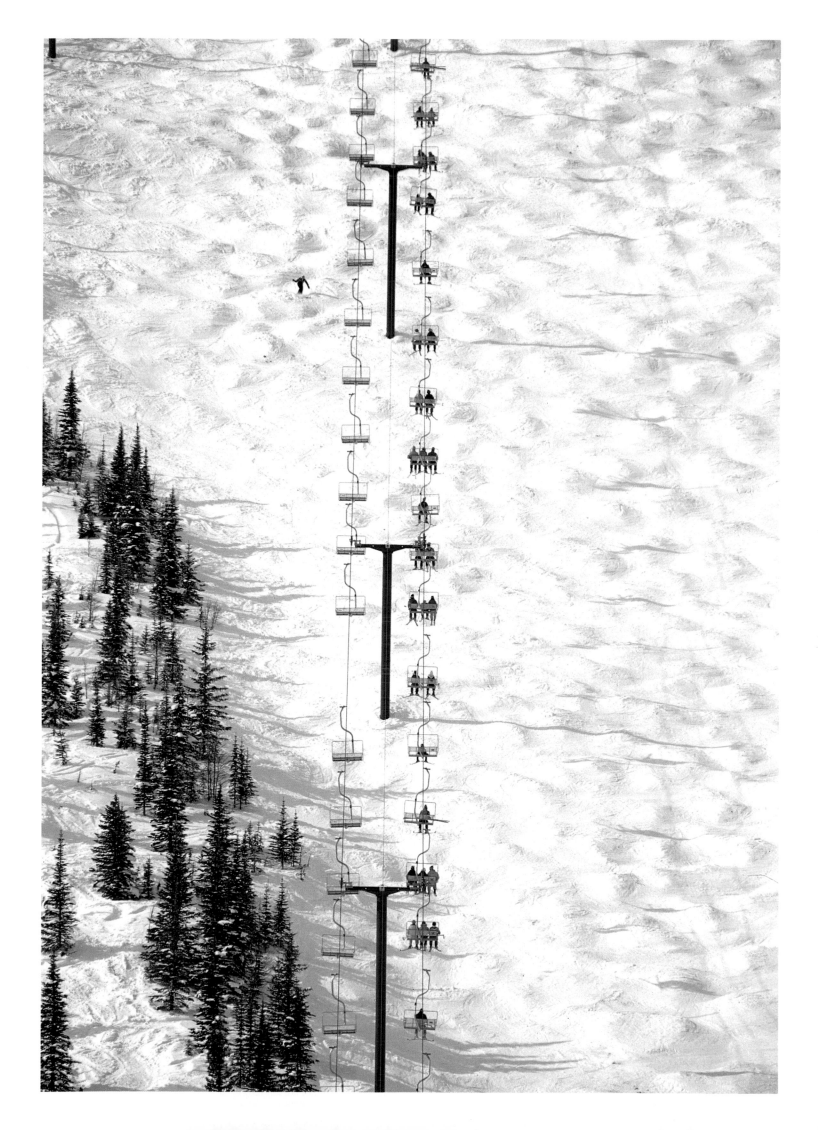

The ski sport continued to enrich its heritage in the early seventies. Even American beauty queens gave it a try. Said Miss Bountiful of Bountiful, Utah, "Next to working as a dental assistant, I like skiing best." Rebecca King, Miss America 1973, who learned to ski at Park City, Utah, revealed that she was sticking with her original goal "to open a law office in a small town that's close to good skiing." The U.S. Ski Wax Company perfumed its downhill line of ski waxes in an effort to get Alpine ski waxes into popular use; red was scented wild cherry, green was lime, silver was cinnamon, blue was sandalwood, and gold was honeysuckle. Jean-Claude Killy won the U.S. pro tour and became the first skier to win all four of skiing's top crowns—the World Cup, the FIS World Championship, the Winter Olympics, and the Pro Championship— skiing's first grand slam. Sitting out the next season with an ulcer, Killy saw Austrian barber–pro racer Hugo Nindl walk off with $93,000 in prize money. Undaunted, Killy added to his fortunes by gamboling in bed in the buff with his wife for *Oui* magazine. Mickey Cochran, father and coach of the fabulous Cochran kids, was named head coach of the U.S. Ski Team but quit in midseason. SKI revealed that among skiers with the worst equipment were orthopedic surgeons. Only three percent (compared to thirty percent of the general ski population) had antifriction pads on their skis, and most orthopedists' equipment was found to be ill adjusted or hopelessly out of date. The editors reasoned that the orthopedists were probably too busy to read the ski magazines and instead got their information from out-of-date medical journals. In 1968 jumper John Bower became the first American to win the Holmenkollen combined, capturing the Kings Cup, skiing's most prestigious trophy. Quebec's Saint Jovite school administration instituted skiing classes at Gray Rocks ski area and within three years found that the percentage of youngsters who failed to graduate went from twenty-nine percent to three percent. President Allende of Chile, doubtless aware of Saint Jovite's success in building better youngsters through skiing, started a program of ski instruction for two hundred poor Santiago families as part of the socialization of Chile. Hunter Mountain, New York, informed by its insurance company that "long hair, unbundled, is a lift-accident hazard," weighed the appropriateness of such warnings as "Don't Let Your Hair Down" and "Hair Today, Gone Tomorrow." Pay-As-You-Ski, a ski-package plan for financing everything from clothing and equipment to a winter holiday, was introduced by Pacific National Bank. Bob Lange, inventor of the plastic ski boot, hit the headlines again, this time for "aiding and abetting a minor to deceive officials of the Soap Box Derby." Lange, ever the tinkerer, had designed an electromagnetic device for the nose of his nephew's soap box that would help it get off to a faster start. "Little John" Truden, defending champion at 475 pounds, was trounced by Terry Tyler, at a slim 440, during the Heavyweight Skiing Championships at Sugarloaf Mountain, Maine. And Dr. Sol Rosenthal, professor of preventive medicine at the University of Illinois, endorsed skiing as one of life's most beneficent risk sports, claiming, "Risk exercise is not only a basic evolutionary need, but it gives exquisite joy and vigor. It helps us maintain our sense of humor, perspective, and, on the evidence I have found, also

Powder, familiar to the Rocky Mountain skier, is no stranger to Quebec. Below, a Canadian threesome cavorts in the deep on Le Massif at Baie Saint Paul.

Opposite and below: *The backcountry, like the terrain you'll find in the high mountains near Whistler in British Columbia, has always been a skier's silent siren—glistening snow, spectacular massifs, an azure sky, suspended moments, and memories that live forever.*

Below: *You never know what you'll run into while skiing, as this young skier on a made-for-kids trail at Aspen discovers.*

Bottom left: *Skiing in New York's Central Park is not only tough, without snow it's downright impossible.*

Bottom right: *Skiers who refuse to point their skis downhill usually become the victims of ski-base ice up, requiring the pole-point scrape of a companion skier. Mount Tom at Holyoke, Massachusetts*

You wouldn't have found the word "snow farming" in the skier's vocabulary forty years ago. Nor would you have found the implements to make and till the snow. In the late sixties and early seventies, snowmaking and snow grooming were elevated to both art and science.

Below: *Snow grooming at Bromley, Vermont*

Bottom: *Snowmaking at Shawnee, Pennsylvania*

With new ski areas springing from the northern Rockies (Wyoming's Grand Targhee, above) to the southern Appalachians (Beech Mountain, North Carolina, opposite), the mark of a skier who'd really been around became his collection of ski patches.

Opposite: *Last run. There's no better season cap than a trek and ski in spring in the backcountry—as these skiers, climbing up Skillet Glacier near Jackson Hole, Wyoming, can tell you.*

Below: *The rites of spring in New Hampshire on Mount Washington's Tuckerman Ravine. No lifts for an assist, it's strictly pay before you play.*

Après-ski today comes in a variety of forms—tennis, swimming, Jacuzzi, aerobics. Even so, the close-order activity for which the term was invented, and which its practitioners demonstrate so capably here, still reigns as number one.

Opposite, above: *Warm times, warm friends at Gray Rocks, Quebec*

Opposite, below: *Whole lot of shakin' in the Boiler Room at Sun Valley*

Below: *The belly-to-belly bar scene at Hunter Mountain, New York*

appreciably improves the participant's sex life.'' With that, *Playboy* magazine's Hugh Hefner announced that a five-million-dollar ski resort would be built near Lake Geneva, Wisconsin. The new area, he claimed, would feature bunnies of all types—snow bunnies as well as lifeguard bunnies—plus an eighteen-hole golf course, ski hill, and 150-room hotel.

Elsewhere on the resort front, Canada built its first aerial lift, a four-passenger gondola at Parc Mont Sainte-Anne in the Laurentians of Quebec. Snowmass, Colorado, opened to raves—''the most glamorous, gorgeous, the most splendidly various of all Aspen's belles,'' wrote one ski writer. The highest lift-served skiing in the East was announced at, of all places, Beech Mountain, North Carolina—elevation 5,600 feet. Alaska, aiming to put itself on the map as a major ski state, told of major development plans for Mount Alyeska. Hawaii, also caught with ski fever, erected a lift on the 13,800-foot

volcano Mauna Kea. Vail introduced snowmaking in Colorado, admitting that "Colorado's Rockies occasionally do have their snow drought problems." Cheboygan, Michigan, opened the world's first—and only remaining—ski hill built from sawdust, a four-acre pile abandoned to the city by a defunct lumber mill. Robert Kronowitt, a Philadelphia kitchen designer, announced plans for what he claimed would be "Skiing's Tower of Babel"—a 250-foot tower with an elevator-like lift in the central shaft. The tower would subtend five refrigerated snow-covered ski chutes from 1,400 feet to half a mile in length, spiraling down from the top landings on the tower like the arms of a whirling octopus. Alec Cushing instituted a "courtesy patrol" on his slopes at Squaw Valley, its job "to go around being helpful and smiling a lot." And Hans Thorner, the crusty owner of Magic Mountain, Vermont, claimed that "eastern skiing, let's face it, is ten good days. The rest is skating!" Ever the iconoclast, Thorner tossed other brickbats: "Unless a major area, any major ski area, has some wait on the lift line on every good snow weekend of the season, it cannot make ends meet.... This is the worst business in the world. Anyone who goes into it has rocks in his head.... The attraction of skiing? Where else can you dress up like a clown and be admired for it?"

Not everyone agreed with Thorner. In fact, few often did. What most did agree on was that skiing was on the frontier of yet another era. Ski areas could no longer be thrown together willy-nilly with a lift here, a hotel there, based on an owner's or financier's whim. With community sensitivities, environmental restrictions, and the huge capital outlays required to fulfill the planning process and build the kind of resort that America's skiers had come to expect, ski-area building required more—much more. And in the next decade it would be the large corporations with limitless resources, rather than the colorful veterans of the postwar ski development era, that would deliver it.

FASHION

Film stars Dick Powell and June Allyson at Sun Valley

Below: *Gretchen Fraser, in slalom action at Sun Valley in 1938, was the epitome of ski fashion in baggy wool knickers, head bandana, and short, belted wool jacket. As simple as ski clothing was in the 1936–45 era,* *equipment—wood skis, lace-up boots, long-thong bindings (bottom and opposite, above)—was even more basic.*

Opposite, below: *Walter Prager (left) and Alf Engen, coaches for the U.S. Ski Team in 1947, helped design these poplin cross-country racing uniforms. The headbands, also part of the uniform, let the wearer's hair flow stylishly free.*

Left: *Boiled wool jacket ($36), matching stretch pants ($50), and zippered turtleneck ($6) were a hot ensemble in the late fifties and early sixties. They were a far cry from the forties' one-piece suit with fly-covered button front and drop-seat rear.*

Below: *The omnifarious turtleneck, introduced in the fifties, was perfect for layering under sweaters. It also served to accentuate a skier's tan.*

Above: *The Mod look arrives. Psyche-delic brights, in-the-boot pants, and op-art treatments set the skiwear trend in the sixties.*

Right: *The sweater-girl look, also from the sixties, never failed to impress skiers of the opposite sex.*

Opposite, left: *Another version of the Mod look, here in the form of long, belted "tow coats," domed hat, and stretch brights*

Opposite, right: *Stretch was the rage in sixties ski fashion. This outfit, in tomato red, was photographed with a Twiggy-look camera angle to accentuate the suit's long, clean silhouette.*

Below: *Sixties ski sweaters were heavy on textures, patterns, and acid colors. It was skiing's Age of Aquarius.*

Right: *The fat-but-functional "down look" marked ski jackets of the early seventies. As fashion moved into the eighties, the treatment for women became more feminine (below). Very Victorian, this jacket, with its high-tech Sontique insulation, was also very warm.*

In the mid-eighties designers experimented with color blocking—big and bold on top, skinny at the bottom.

Below left: *The over-the-boot gaitered pant, topped off by a nylon pullover, was a popular look in the early eighties.*

Below right: *Earth tones appeared briefly in the eighties, along with a looser silhouette that replaced the body-hugging performance look.*

Left: *Back to the future? Beginning in the seventies, new fabrics and new insulations gave rise to new interpretations on the forties look; this adaptation is a throwback to the era of the short, belted jacket with wide lapels.*

Below: *As skiwear looked back, it also leaped forward. This high-tech twosome shows the way, with ultrathin insulations (Gore-Tex, Mylar, Thinsulate) that give more skiing freedom and a tailored silhouette.*

Opposite, left: *Pretty pastels in water-proof, breathable fabrics were a sign of the times in the eighties.*

Opposite, right: *Cotton one-piece suits, hand painted or factory filigreed, became the mark of the eighties skier. With the utilitarian look fading, skiwear became bright, happy clothing to play in.*

Below: *Another version of the short, belted forties look, reinterpreted in eye-catching color for the skier of today*

PART V
THE AGE OF
SEASONING

There are things that concern me about skiing. . . . It doesn't need hype, affectation. There's a whole shopping-mall kind of mentality that's taken over. We've gone too fast. We've pushed too hard to create an image, spent too much money on building those aspects of skiing that are just not important to the skier.

—Robert Redford, SKI Magazine, November 1975

The ski sport had grown quickly in the United States—some would say too quickly—when we came to look back upon ourselves in the year of America's Bicentennial. In four short decades we had established effective learning techniques, pioneered in trail maintenance and design, created snowmaking, led the world in resort development, innovated with major equipment advances, and staged a successful Winter Olympics. Were there any fields left to conquer?

Yes. Americans have always been known as an enterprising, showboating lot, so it was not unexpected that the 1976–86 period would hold a few surprises of its own. It was no matter that America's wonderful winter pastime would encounter occasional setbacks and stumbling blocks. Skiing would endure, with all the flash and dazzle that had marked its earlier years.

Firsts? There were plenty of them—some valiant, some bordering on the lunatic. Frank Bare, on skis, popped a triple twisting quadruple flip—four back flips with three full twists—a stunt filmmaker Dick Barrymore called "the most incredible athletic maneuver I've ever witnessed." Skier-mountaineer Chris Landry skied the east face of Aspen's Pyramid Peak from the summit, considered an impossible descent. Joe Flick and his Fabulous Flippers went hand-in-hand into the record books with the first seventeen-man back flip on skis. Italian instructors Matteo Thun and Giorgio Ferraris skied the sulphur-choked lava flanks of Stromboli as the volcano erupted, happy that "although our ski bases had melted, our edges still held." Harry Slutter and Robert Smith set a joint downhill skiing record of 102 hours, with Smith skiing backward. Skier-mountaineer Ned Gillette and his team of four became the first humans to circle Mount Everest on skis. And Charlie Nebel, at the age of eighty-two, skied a million vertical feet in eleven weeks at Jackson Hole; his wife, Dot, skied with him but couldn't claim a record because she had lost track of her runs.

There were other records, like that of lanky, long-haired Californian Steve McKinney, who in 1978 shattered skiing's 200 kilometer-per-hour barrier with a blistering 124.34 miles-per-hour run, the equivalent of traveling the length of a football field in 1.8 seconds. McKinney set his record at Portillo, Chile, high in the Andes. The track was steep and long, beginning with a forty-degree pitch at the top and gradually, after 3,412 feet, flattening below. It was a superb speed track, one in which high speeds were reached quickly.

Roll your own! Or nine ways to change your mind on how to make a landing. Freestyle aerials, perversely, in the eighties moved from the ridiculous to the sublime, from hotdog brash to Olympic respectability.

McKinney's triumph gave new respectability, and new exposure, to speed skiing. For one, speed skiers were different—a little cosmic, a little poetic, a lot into self-discovery. Said McKinney after setting the Portillo speed record:

> I find that the faster my body travels the slower my mind seems to work. What seems like an eternity to calculate a movement actually passes almost instantaneously until finally at the crescendo of speed there is no thought at all. It is simply a case of reflex, instinct, and faith. . . . Faith? Sometimes we must defer our thirst for scientific proof to acceptance of something deeper. When we don't know, we must trust in the wisdom of God's plan. The moments before the plunge to a speed record are moments full of this trust. To go without it is literally to take your life in your hands.

Skiing, in the fast-paced seventies, had other adventurous spirits, such as instructor Joe Meegan, who skied a frozen Niagara Falls. Coach Dan Quinlan set a cross-country time-and-distance record by skiing 174 miles in twenty-four hours, averaging 7.25 miles per hour in the attempt. Kirk Hill set the world single-skier endurance record at Angel Fire, New Mexico, by completing 434 consecutive runs covering 195,300 vertical feet, skiing nonstop for sixty-three hours, fifty minutes until he "began losing contact with reality." Tiny Liechtenstein (population 25,000) produced four 1980 Olympic medals, two World Cup champions in Hanni and Andreas Wenzel, a national hangover, and a new meaning for the term "small wonder."

Finally, there was the Swiss daredevil-adventurer Sylvain Saudan, who climbed up without oxygen and skied down 26,470-foot Hidden Peak in the Himalayas, the highest descent ever on skis. The record cost him $300,000, required 225 sherpas and high-altitude porters, and took nine hours in a descent over 9,000 vertical feet, during which Saudan made more than 3,000 turns over slopes of fifty to fifty-five degrees in steepness in conditions that he described as "the absolute worst I have ever skied." Why did he do it? "Adventure," said Saudan. "Besides, why not ski down if you take the trouble to climb up?"

This spirit of derring-do, of go for broke, was brought spectacularly to the ski scene in 1976 by a twenty-three-year-old farm boy from Mooswald, Austria, by the name of Franz Klammer. Klammer's gold-medal run in the downhill at the Innsbruck Winter Olympics, seen by the world on television, was on-the-edge drama at its best.

Klammer, determined to beat longtime Swiss rival Bernhard Russi, had trouble initially on the upper part of the Patscherkofel course, then—after posting the third-best intermediate time—he went all out. Nearly airborne with one leg stretched out to retain contact with the snow, the other knee raised high and hugging his chest to fight off air resistance, Klammer was able to hold his line better than anyone else in the last turn before the final schuss. It was a spectacular

The ski sport, competitively and recreationally, took a variety of directions in the eighties. Women, for the first time, started setting records in speed skiing (below). Monoskiing (opposite, above), popular in the Alps, started to catch on in the United States. Skiing traditionalists regarded it as dementia.

Opposite, below: Sylvain Saudan, Swiss daredevil on skis, takes the plunge from 26,470 feet in the Himalayas. It was another first in an era of firsts.

Opposite: *Western resorts gained a reputation not only for abundant snow but for terrain that could test the reflexes of the best. One of the best tests of the best was, and still is, Jackson Hole, Wyoming.*

performance, relived in the conversations of New York cab drivers and Seattle sanitation workers, in Boston bars and on California beaches.

The same Olympics saw other moments: Rosi Mittermaier's down-to-the-wire rush for three gold medals, her record thwarted in the giant slalom by Canada's Kathy Kreiner; and Bill Koch's silver in the Nordic 30-kilometer, the first American Olympic Nordic medal ever. Koch's spectacular performance would usher in a new era for American ski racing, culminating in U.S. Olympic, World Championship, and World Cup victories throughout the decade and touching off a recreational race craze the likes of which had never been witnessed before.

None of this could have happened, of course, if things hadn't become easier. Skiers, reared on GLM and gear that was a cinch to use, got better as the decade progressed. Equipment had come a long way from the days of stiff hickory skis, inefficient bindings, and sloppy leather boots. For one, it was safer. Said Dr. Jake Shealy of the Rochester Institute of Technology in 1976, "The injury rate per thousand-skier days has dropped by fifty percent over the past ten years—and even better days are coming."

Two important developments in bindings appeared: the antifriction device and the widespread use of the ski brake. The antifriction device (AFD), a Teflon pad placed under the toe of the boot sole to reduce friction between boot and ski top, was claimed by designers and users to be "the most important advance in binding design since the release binding was invented." The ski brake finally came to be accepted as a major deterrent in preventing ski injuries. SKI reported, "The proof is in—ski-stopping devices do increase the skier's margin of safety. They could reduce all injuries by eight to ten percent and head injuries by fifty percent."

Ski bindings themselves had become safer through features such as built-in elasticity to prevent premature release, centering force to return the toe to center after minor shocks, and multidirectional release. They were also convenient, with easy step-in, step-out and no-more-bending, hands-off operation.

In boots the trend was toward lighter, simpler, softer, all with the aim of increasing skier comfort and performance. It was an era in which experimentation knew no bounds. Some experiments worked, most did not. The knee-high boot did not. Designed to give the skier greater edging ability and resultant turning power, knee-high boots took the ski sport by storm in 1982. A few seasons later it was found that the boot's rigidity wouldn't allow skiers to bend their ankles. There was also the problem of finding knee-high pants that would work with the boot. Exit the knee-high boot.

Integrated boot and binding systems also appeared. The idea behind this development—from Look/Nordica, Koflach, and Spademan—was that engineers could create a boot sole better suited to the mechanical requirements of the binding. The boot sole could also be made shorter than normal, for easier walking and to enable the ski to flex more fully underfoot.

Other uses for skis, as demonstrated by
their users: climbing Tuckerman Ravine
in New Hampshire (below left), low-al-
titude inverteds at Alpine Meadows,
California (below right), and sky diving
at Emerald Bay in Tahoe, California
(opposite).

Below: *Skis opened up a whole new world for the adventuresome. It was called the backcountry—a nirvana of beauty whose joys and possibilities seemed endless. Bear Valley, California*

Opposite: *A pause that refreshes. The only problem with skiing Oregon's Steens Mountain is missing the views from Steens Mountain while you're skiing it.*

The idea bombed when skiers discovered that an integrated boot wouldn't work with rental skis or skis with conventional bindings. They were also too expensive, selling at a price equivalent to that for boots and bindings separately.

If knee-highs and integrated boot and binding systems were doomed from the start, rear-entry boots were another matter. This design, pioneered by Hanson and later adopted by virtually every boot manufacturer, was a hands-down winner. Rear-entry boots were user friendly, having fewer buckles and no tongue to align, and, with the absence of buckle pressure points, were far more comfortable than traditional overlap-shell designs.

That bootmaking during the period became as much an art as a discipline in engineering was evidenced by *Fortune*'s list of "The 25 Best Designed Products," in which appeared the Hanson Avanti boot, in the company of a Bang & Olufsen stereo, Porsche 911-S Targa sports car, and Enstrom helicopter.

As boots improved, so did skis. Though no one still could quite agree on ski length, there was some consensus on the proper materials for building a ski. Space-age materials like Kevlar, Boron, and graphite were suddenly being combined with exotic damping systems, angled sidewalls, hollow-channel and honeycomb cores, self-sharpening edges, super-fast bases, air spoilers, ridgetops, forked tails, flex adjusters, blunt tips, grooveless bases, and asymmetric sidecuts. And no matter what ski length you preferred—whether a midder, compact lover, sport buff, median skier, or long-ski purist—you were bound to find something that would take you for a ride in style. If price were no object, you could even spring for a ski like the $790 Lacroix—which was bound to impress your friends if not your spouse or banker.

Equipment and technique, of course, have traditionally been intertwined in skiing, so it was not uncommon to refer to one when discussing the other. And opinions varied greatly. Jean-Claude Killy asked in SKI, "Are you a 180-centimeter weakling?" His advice: "Go longer and your skiing will improve *rapidement*!" Whether it was Killy's advice that prompted America to return to long skis as the decade closed is anyone's guess. In any case, the market for short skis, as had that for long skis ten years before, fell out. And to ease the glut of surplus shorties, Ski Industries of America, the industry's trade association, showed America how to turn its short skis into a tax deduction by running them to their local ski shop, where they could be recycled for use by disabled skiers. It was expected, of course, that skiers would then purchase more acceptable-length gear, which they happily proceeded to do. By 1985 sales of ski equipment and apparel had passed the billion-dollar mark.

In apparel no single look characterized the period 1976–86. Rather, there were three: the Racer Look, exemplified by sleek suits, with sausage padding and stretch-action stripes that gave the wearer a fast look even when he was not skiing; the Coordinated Look, in which everything matched—jacket, sweater, gloves, skis, fanny pack, bibs; and the High-Tech Look, with Gore-Tex parka, waterproof/breathable pants, gaiters, Gore-Tex/Thinsulate gloves, and Vuarnet sunglasses.

Given the fact that now things were really rolling in skiwear and equipment, skiers turned their sights to other, less-settled areas of the sport—technique, for example.

The Graduated Length Method of ski instruction, which had spawned a whole new generation of skiers in the sixties, had now been around for a while. So it was not surprising that forward-thinking theoreticians began taking potshots at GLM. Even SKI Magazine, which had helped develop GLM and introduce it to the American public, began to question the method.

In "The Unlearning of GLM" SKI's editors asked, "Are those short skis you learned on keeping you from proper technique on longer skis?" What resulted was a compromise approach developed by the Professional Ski Instructors of America that started beginners on skis slightly longer, a hundred centimeters, then graduated them to more conventional-length skis, one hundred fifty centimeters and longer.

The rewards of high Alpine cross-country skiing are prizes like these: gliding deep on Dewey Point in Yosemite (below left) and early morning on Mount Assiniboine on the border of Alberta and British Columbia (below).

Opposite: *The beauty of cross-country is that you can do it at your own pace. Some prefer the solitude of a leisurely tour; others* (below) *like it fast—sometimes crowded.*

Still, GLM in its purest form continued to have its boosters. Salvaging the klutzy, the uncoordinated, and the underachievers of southern California was the self-proclaimed goal of Art Poland and his Alternative Ski School at Snow Summit, California. Poland, who put his ski school dropouts on short skis, found that eighty-six percent of them could ski solo after only one class.

If GLM had proved it could make Alpine skiers out of never-evers, it was also being tested—under the label GWM (Graduated Width Method)—as an instructional approach in cross-country skiing. It was found that small graduated differences in the width of a cross-country ski could make a big difference in how fast the beginner learned the sport.

Other shibboleths were also being debated. PSIA technical chief Horst Abraham questioned the validity of parallel skiing. "Truly spontaneous skiers," said Abraham, "mix stemmed, stepped, and parallel turn initiations as the situation demands. Although a skier can force himself to use a parallel turn in any situation, he does so with a sacrifice to balance and efficiency—his forced maneuver is plain misinterpretation of a sport rich with options." SKI technical editor Stu Campbell, taking another shot at the feet-together myth, agreed. "If God had intended that we ski with welded feet," said Campbell, "he never would have made skis in pairs."

If such thinking was blasphemy to old-line theoreticians, other experiments also began to rattle the ski teaching establishment. Psychological approaches to ski instruction—Inner Skiing, Skiing through Yoga, Super Learning, Centered Skiing ("challenging not the hips but the head")—were suddenly in. Several were successful in helping skiers overcome their fears and phobias; others, not so successful, concentrated on mind games to the exclusion of basic skiing skills.

New techniques, meanwhile, were surfacing at the sport's more advanced levels. French theoretician Georges Joubert, longtime observer of World Cup racing technique, introduced the "surf" technique. This maneuver, in which the racer rode a flat ski in the turn rather than edging, and braking, throughout the turn, was too complex for most skiers—it required the skier to place his knees and feet to the outside of the turn, a maneuver that some felt was biomechanically impossible.

The A-frame, another racing maneuver, enjoyed better acceptance. With the legs forming an inverted V, or A-frame, from the knees to the feet, one could extend the outside ski, coil the inside leg, and, by pushing the skis and using leverage, better control speed in the turns. The A-frame, claimed its proponents, gave the skier a greater sense of balance, created a steady platform from which to make a turn, and required the skier's body to do less work. It was the kind of exercise that skiers were anxious to know about, particularly in a race-crazy period when everyone was taking to the gates—in club races, sweetheart races, family races, races for chefs, firemen, doctors, seniors, bartenders, and businessmen.

If record numbers of skiers were getting into racing, they were doing it with good reason. The 1976–86 period was the strongest ever for American ski racing. At its close, more than two million skiers had taken part in NASTAR events alone.

Below: *Skiers make the day's last run in the Monashees of British Columbia. Helicopter skiing opened up new frontiers for the powder skier. Others, such as this skier touring in the Canadian Selkirks (opposite), preferred their own backcountry propulsion.*

It had all started in 1978. Phil Mahre, coming off a spectacular season, took an unprecedented second overall in the World Cup, the best international season-long performance ever by an American. He continued with strong results the next season but shattered his ankle at the Lake Placid pre-Olympics, dashing U.S. hopes for its first World Cup and putting Mahre's future as a ski racer in doubt. Miraculously, Mahre not only recovered but went on to win the overall 1981 World Cup, then followed by capturing the 1982 and 1983 World Cups as well. Meanwhile, Phil's twin brother, Steve, the other half of the Dynamic Duo from White Pass, Washington, took the gold medal in giant slalom, six weeks after major knee surgery, at the 1982 FIS Alpine World Championships. The American women, led by Tamara McKinney, Christin Cooper, and Cindy Nelson, skied to a first place in the Nations Cup the same season. The next year Phil Mahre and Tamara McKinney won the men's and women's overall World Cup. In doing so, they had at long last achieved the impossible:

Opposite: *The 1980 Winter Olympics. Lake Placid, New York, site of the 1932 Winter Games, became the first North American resort to host a Winter Olympics twice. Two events that had been added to the Winter Games since 1932 were the biathlon (above) and the downhill (below).*

Page 198: *Ski jumping, always a crowd thriller, drew throngs of spectators in 1980 at Lake Placid. The seventy-meter and ninety-meter events were, as usual, dominated by Scandinavians and eastern Europeans.*

Page 199: *Pro racing, head-to-head parallel competition down a course strewn with tight gates and jumps, is a far cry from the one-racer-against-the-clock format of World Cup racing. An arduous competition requiring up to a dozen runs down the course to earn a day's win, the tour has drawn a number of former World Cup and Olympic stars over the years.*

America, a non-Alpine country and traditional nonpower in international ski racing, had broken the European stranglehold on the sport.

But the Americans were just warming up. As 1984 rolled around, expectations were high. The U.S. team was strong, stronger than it had ever been in history, with potential for several Olympic gold medals. And gold medals are what the Americans won. Debbie Armstrong, from Seattle, was first, with a gold in the women's giant slalom; teammate Christin Cooper took the silver. Downhiller Bill Johnson, brash and testy, predicted that the only race would be for second place, went out and won the Olympic downhill, then announced modestly, "I don't know why the other guys bothered to show up." Phil and Steve Mahre skied one-two in the slalom, then learned that Phil had become a father the same day. America's 1984 Olympic medal count went to five, including an unprecedented three golds.

With all the hoopla over the U.S. performance at Sarajevo, most overlooked a group of American youngsters standing in the wings. But not for long. The following year, in the 1985 FIS Alpine World Championships, the world saw Americans capture four more medals—three bronzes and a gold—and the flawless giant slalom performance of Diann Roffe, a seventeen-year-old from Rochester, New York. Roffe, whom coaches had expected to win a medal at the *Junior* World Championships two weeks later—became not only the first American woman to win a World Championship gold medal but the youngest racer ever to do so. Bronze medals, for third-place finishes, were also won by team newcomers Doug Lewis in the downhill and Eva Twardokens in giant slalom, and by veteran Tamara McKinney in the combined.

While American ski racers were busy collecting medals, the recreational skier continued to wrestle with the task of making turns. But England's Lady Diana Spencer, betrothed to Prince Charles, seemed not the least confused over the issue of proper ski technique, explaining hers as simply "going downhill as fast as I can and never turning." As for the sport's beginners, many were still trying to cope with the basic terminology of the sport. Morten Lund, longtime ski writer, instructor, and observer of skiing's pratfalls, tried to make things easier by defining some terms in SKI:

Fall   *A sincere attempt to slow down*

Turn   *The act of avoiding other skiers by attempting to zig when they zag, a futile strategy ultimately doomed to spectacular failure, recrimination, and bruised egos*

Snowplow   *A spirited position requiring sprung hip sockets, steel hamstrings, and quadriceps to die for*

Opposite: *Sweden's Ingemar Stenmark, with a little help from silver medalist Phil Mahre* (right) *and bronze medalist Jacques Luethy of Switzerland, goes aloft after winning slalom gold at Lake Placid.*

Boots   *Traditional skiing footwear, extraordinarily unyielding, designed to develop and penetrate blisters, create bone spurs, and make eyes water; principal cause of psychopathic behavior on the slopes*

Instructor   *Catlike creature with mirrored sunglasses and sunlamp tan, most at ease with humans of the opposite sex; can be flushed out of ski school shack and forced to give ski lessons by threatening deprivation of all caffeine and nicotine for sixty minutes*

Rules of the road   *Precepts to be obeyed in order to ensure safety on the slopes. Main rules: 1) the first skier to the intersection gets hit from behind, 2) four skiers together in the middle of a trail can make other skiers go around them, 3) of two converging skiers, the heavier, faster skier has the right of way, 4) stopping short above another skier and spraying him with snow makes him a wimp*

Lift lines   *Game of guile and politics with the object of moving ahead of people who have lined up before you arrived*

Fall line   *Narrow furrow straight downhill made by the nose of a fallen skier*

Expert slope   *Any terrain on which the skier falls more than once*

Meanwhile, the world of skiing careened on. Coin-operated hot air blowers to warm boots were installed in two hundred U.S. ski resorts. President Gerald Ford blamed his 1976 election loss on a lack of skiers, claiming, "We carried almost every state in which skiing is important. Our problem was that we didn't have enough skiers." The Associated Press, United Press International, and *People* magazine ran photos of oil sheik Saleim Abdul Haddad skiing at Winter Park, Colorado, only to learn later that the sheik was really George Haddad, a shoe dealer from Duluth. The first skier elected pope, John Paul II, said, "I will ski again when they let me." Stuart Caren of Boulder, Colorado, was issued a $15 citation for skiing a closed run at Taos, New Mexico. He forgot about it, then fought it, then ended up paying a fine of $50 plus $500 in court costs.

Another skier who paid handsomely for his little flight of fancy was Vermont realtor Bob McKee. A skier from Stowe who had tried ski racing for the first time at the age of thirty, the thirty-nine-year-old McKee convinced the Irish Ski Federation,

without the funds to field a racer let alone an entire ski team, to allow him to race for Ireland in World Cup competition. Six months, 22,500 miles, 38 races, and $7,000 later, McKee had become an anti-hero, adored by the European press as the Irish team's only coach, trainer, service technician, and financial backer—in every sense of the word the only true "amateur" on the World Cup circuit. By far the slowest, and oldest, of the World Cup downhillers, McKee lamented, "Most guys my age were worrying about their hairlines and waistlines, and here I was worrying about whether I was going to get killed."

Writing about the experience later, McKee reported, "At Val d'Isère the race jury told me they were kicking me out of the race. I was too slow. I told them I was just 'testing skis.' I was then humiliated in three different languages as the jury explained to the other team captains why the Irish racer and team captain was so slow."

McKee's tenacity paid off when, during the Alpine combined event of the Arlberg-Kandahar, one of the most prestigious of Alpine ski races, he came in third to win the bronze. No matter that only three racers finished the event, McKee's name still went into the record book. Said McKee after the race, "I bet this is the last year they give this award."

Back in the United States, ski life went on. Pro skier Spider Sabich died from gunshot wounds inflicted by singer-companion Claudine Longet. Amy Carter, the president's daughter, learned to ski at Crested Butte, Colorado; the president's brother, Billy, did the same at Telemark, Wisconsin, and reported, "I froze my tail off." Lift-tower billboards, advertising everything from soup to sun cream, appeared at eastern ski resorts, much to the annoyance of skiers who claimed they skied to escape such things. Computers came to ski buying; skiers had only to tell where they skied, how well they skied, how fast they skied, and the computer told them which skis, boots, and bindings to buy. New York, with 218 ski areas, announced it was "the ski-craziest state of all."

Craziest *skier* of all was Rick Sylvester, whose parachute jump with skis off the top of Yosemite's El Capitan in 1973 had put him indelibly into skiing's daredevil hall of fame. Sylvester was a hot item, the kind of stunter most studios would give their sound stage for. The producer of the James Bond films convinced Sylvester to leap for Bond in the opening scenes of *The Spy Who Loved Me.* And leap he did, with parachute and skis, off the top of three-thousand-foot Mount Asgard on Canada's Baffin Island. The sport, in pursuit of the ultimate in derring-do, had hit an all-time high.

In other developments, Dr. Lynn England of Brigham Young University found that skiers were happier than ordinary people. Other of Dr. England's findings: skiers were against snowmobiles and skating rinks but in favor of nightclubs, bars, and liquor stores. Club Med made its debut in the American ski world at Copper Mountain, Colorado. Cedar Rapids, Iowa, inspired by Mount Trashmore, Illinois, accumulated one million tons of garbage to build its own ski hill. Paoli Peaks,

Indiana, announced a midnight-to-6:00 A.M. lift ticket for local meat packers. Vail, Colorado, instituted a get-tough policy for skiers who ignored "Trail Closed" signs: six months in jail and a $500 fine. Ralph Lauren unveiled the perfect solution to skiing's cold-weather woes: an all-mink ski parka priced at $3,500. Brandywine, Ohio, unveiled the world's first eight-passenger chair lift, which was actually two quadruple chairs synchronized as one. Colorado reported that despite skier gripes over lift-ticket costs, "only a small portion of a ski vacation budget goes for uphill transportation." Aside from the airfare costs to reach Colorado's resorts, said the state's area association, skiers spent most on "retail purchases" ($202 million), indicating that skiers spend more off the mountain than on.

The resort scene changed dramatically between 1976 and 1986. As the period began, the life of the ski area operator was anything but rosy. First, the environmental era had taken its toll. It had begun in 1969 with Disney's ill-fated Mineral King project, an ambitious California winter playground no sooner proposed than it hit the skids, the victim of environmental hammerlock. With the subsequent passage of the National Environmental Policy Act and the establishment of the Environmental Protection Agency, it became virtually impossible to develop new ski facilities on U.S. Forest Service land, where most Rocky Mountain and Sierra resorts were and are located. Adding to the problems of Vermont's ski area operators was the passage of Act 250, an environmental code that severely limited the building and expansion of ski areas in the state.

To be sure, some area operators had brought these strictures upon themselves by throwing up hastily conceived "improvements," cluttering area access roads, and polluting mountain streams and air. The result was that responsible area

Opposite: Racer ready . . . go! All competitors today use the "Killy start," originated by the French triple-Olympic-gold-medal winner. The move begins with an explosive pole push to launch the upper body downhill, ahead of the feet, which are the last part of the body to trip the starting wand. With downhill momentum already underway before the clock is activated, the racer can gain valuable fractions of a second in the start.

Below: To the victors go the spoils. The season-long World Cup, a grueling series of races played out on courses throughout the world, is not well known to the American public, but it is a national team racer's mainstay. The crystal World Cup, to a ski racer, surpasses even Olympic gold.

developers, who were in the majority, found themselves hamstrung by paperwork, protracted approval processes, and the adversarial maneuvering of local preservationist groups.

Adding to all this was the "great wilderness grab" of 1978—known more formally as RARE-II (Roadless Area Review and Evaluation). Under RARE-II the government announced that it was setting aside 187 million acres of public land for reassessment and determination of its future status. RARE-II effectively put a further lock on ski area development. SKI Magazine asked its readers to write to their congressmen, urging reapportionment of RARE-II land for recreational use. The campaign apparently had its effect: the best sites for potential ski area development were ultimately saved and assigned to nonwilderness designation. The input from the public—"the biggest response ever received by any federal agency except the Census Bureau," said the U.S. Forest Service—favored multiple use of the wilderness by a resounding three-to-one margin.

*America's Steve Mahre (opposite), to-
gether with brother Phil (below), created the greatest one-two punch in
American ski racing history. The twins
capped their career, stylishly, with slalom silver (Steve) and gold (Phil) at Sarajevo in 1984.*

Bill Johnson—bad, brash, ultimate victim of post-Olympic burnout—was America's first male Olympic gold medal winner. Said a confident Johnson before his Olympic downhill win, "The only race here is for second place." The comment did not sit well with others of his specialty.

No sooner had the sport dressed its wounds from RARE-II than it was hit with another bombshell. A skier, James Sunday, injured after falling on a trail at Stratton Mountain, Vermont, sued the resort and was awarded $1.5 million. The traditional defense that the skier assumed the risk was suddenly eliminated. The Vermont Supreme Court ruled the defense "no longer appropriate" since, in the court's view, ski resorts had changed—and in the case of trail conditions, presumably for the better.

The result was the beginning of a period of skyrocketing ski area insurance costs and, with them, lift-ticket prices. Ski areas saw their insurance premiums suddenly jump twenty to four hundred percent. Said one operator, echoing the sentiments of others, "The liability thing is unreal. It assumes we can control the elements and turn everything into a nice, neat sandbox. Hell, that's nature out there!"

As if the liability crisis wasn't enough to make area operators wonder why they ever got into the business, Mother Nature was determined to get her licks in as well. The 1976–77 season brought a snow drought to the Rockies. Snow was so scarce, in fact, that Colorado Governor Lamm declared the state a disaster area. After a staggering $78 million loss that ski season, Colorado voted $300,000 for cloud seeding "just in case." State officials did admit that cloud seeding tended to produce another ten to fifteen percent in snow volume "when it was going to snow anyway, but it doesn't do a damn thing if it wasn't." Hit in 1981 with its second drought in four years, Colorado finally bit the bullet, tipped its hat to the East, where area operators had learned how to deal with snowless winters, and invested $15 million in snowmaking equipment.

It was obvious, by the middle of the decade, that building and running ski resorts had become a serious business. In the heyday of the sixties, there were more than 1,400 ski areas in the United States. By 1977 the number had dropped to fewer than 1,000. As this is written, the count is 680.

What happened? What *is* happening?

Given the financial resources required to build a ski area today—to meet the costs of prolonged approval processes, liability, building codes, high borrowing rates, and a capital investment that can be amortized over only six months of the year at best—it has become easier to buy, or to consolidate, than to build. This accounts for the entry into the ski business of such large corporations as Ralston-Purina (Keystone, Arapahoe Basin), Twentieth Century-Fox (Aspen Mountain, Buttermilk, Snowmass, Breckenridge), the Gillett Group (Vail, Beaver Creek), and Little America (Sun Valley, Snowbasin). It also accounts for the recent takeovers and acquisitions of smaller areas by larger resorts. The day of the lone, enterprising Tenth Mountain Division veteran, with his love for the sport and his contagious commitment to creating a resort and making it work, is long since past.

Below: *Franz (the Kaiser) Klammer was skiing's first television ski racing star. His on-the-brink performance in the down-hill at Innsbruck in 1976 was sports drama at its best.*

Opposite: *America's Cindy Nelson, a dedicated and feisty competitor who won Olympic downhill bronze at Inns-bruck in 1976, competed on the U.S. Ski Team for eleven years.*

But, you might ask, isn't it possible to build a *small* area, without the frills, and make it go? SKI Magazine asked the same question in 1978 in the article "Anyone for a Bargain-Basement Ski Resort?" The answer, based on interviews with resort planners, area operators, marketing experts, and Joe Skier: "After dining on caviar, who wants to go back to grits?" Another way of putting that was posed by SKI in the article "Where Have All the Small Areas Gone?" Answered small-area operators, "We're still here—but where have all the skiers gone?"

The truth was that skiers, despite their public clamor over the escalating cost of skiing, wanted "more" and "better." And the nation's ski resorts delivered, with high-capacity snowmaking plants, faster, more sophisticated lifts, high-tech grooming equipment, sumptuous base facilities, and new services to make the skier's life all the more comfortable.

As the resort scene changed, so did skier attitudes. Skiing now had a history—albeit a short one—and as we sat back to reflect on it all, some things became evident. For one, some thought that skiing was becoming *too* comfortable, that we

Ski racing arrives in South America. When the World Cup opened in Argentina in August 1985, the season got off to an early start. Ski racing, and skiing, had come a long way in fifty years. Here, America's Debbie Armstrong comes out of the starting gate.

were striving for a Utopia that was neither attainable nor desirable, and that maybe "the way it was" was better after all.

Rigo Thurmer, skier-architect-mountaineer and a SKI Magazine contributor, brought home the point in his 1978 article "The Quality of the Ski Experience":

> "Convenience" seems to be the magic new ingredient of our lives. Cradle to grave, we are assaulted by it; there's hardly anything left that's not convenient anymore. Naturally, ski areas are hard pressed to jump on the bandwagon. They are expected to make skiing convenient for every functional illiterate who shows up at the ticket window. . . . We might just have to remember what skiing was all about in the first place. Skiing was about discovery, like finding a new line down the mountain. It was about adventure, like skiing through the woods and not knowing where you'd come out. It was about challenge, like reading the conditions of a steep gully right and not having it avalanche. Deep down, that spirit is still alive in most of us. . . . To be sure, we cannot turn skiing back into the Utopia of the twenties, but we can prevent skiing from turning into an Orwellian machine that will ultimately spell the end of the sport we love. . . . But maybe the renaissance of skiing isn't in the cards anymore. Maybe we are too far gone down the road of sanitized toilet seats, diapered minds, and twenty-four-hour protection and will continue to press for more and more comfort, convenience, and . . . a thirty-five-dollar lift ticket to support it all.

Not all skiers, of course, were as critical as Thurmer. In fact, most thought the sport was doing quite well, thank you. And that included luminaries from the fields of literature, religion, and entertainment, a population that was being drawn to skiing in increasing numbers each year.

Said the late novelist John Cheever, "Skiing is an intense pleasure. I even like people I meet in lift lines. In fact, I can't think of anything I don't like about skiing."

Skiing, for songwriter John Denver, "is inspiration. It fills all your senses—it fills everything!"

Pope John Paul II, who explained that his one luxury in life was a pair of Head skis, lamented, "I wish I could be out there somewhere in the mountains, racing down into the valley. It's an extraordinary sensation."

Novelist Leon Uris settled in Aspen to be close to the sport: "There is enormous beauty and serenity in skiing. It revitalizes me as a writer."

Finally, the late Truman Capote confessed, "I have the perfect body for skiing. I can do just about anything on skis. I have a certain element of—well, courage, really."

As we find ourselves on the threshold of another new era in American skiing, where, as the saying goes, do we go from here?

Like raised and lowered hemlines and all things else in life, skiing has come full cycle. And like the doddering old man, we are starting to repeat ourselves. The telemark turn, the accepted method of maneuvering a pair of skis before parallel skiing showed us another way, has returned to be practiced and ballyhooed by the young. Freestyle skiing, which started with a bang and then sputtered, is on the comeback with the promise of becoming a spectacular Olympic event. The ridge-top ski, a rakish design of the forties, has now returned in a fiberglass reincarnation. Backcountry skiing—hiking rather than riding up for the descent, skiing the snow the way you find it rather than the way the area packs it—is now being pursued as a reminder of how our grandfathers skied. Clothing is returning to the casual, baggy look—led by, of all designers, Bogner, the company that created the svelte, streamlined look.

Despite the sport's ups and downs, its foibles and its glories, there is no reason to doubt that skiing's next fifty years will be every bit as rowdy, adventurous, spectacular, and ascendant as its first.

Just ask Robert Redford, who led this chapter with his thoughts on skiing as we approached the last decade and who, at the close of skiing's first fifty years, remarked, "Where else can you get such a collection of bodies smiling? And feeling good about it? And that to me is worth it—to see older people, younger people, just having a ball, just enjoying this fantastic sport in their own way. . . . The sport is smiling through."

R E S O R T S

Aspen aglow. It's called the Winternational, a week of World Cup activity and town events that culminate with a fireworks display on Aspen Mountain.

Skiing in Quebec (large photograph) *has its own abundant rewards—fun trails* (Camp Fortune in Gatineau Park, be-low, inset), *fabulous cookery, and French-Canadian charm* (Mont Trem-blant, opposite, inset).

Faces of Vermont. Whether skirting a glade at Sugarbush (left), tackling Stowe's notorious Front Four (below), or skiing it easy at Bolton Valley (opposite), the experience is New England skiing at its very best.

Opposite: *Stately extremes. Jay Peak in northern Vermont (above) and Killington in the south-central part of the state (below) are not only miles apart geographically, they also attract a different, but equally devoted, skiing breed.*

Midwest hills like Spirit Mountain, Minnesota (bottom), may not be able to compete in vertical feet with areas like Pico, Vermont (below), but their skiers can compete, pound for pound in enthusiasm, with the best.

Northeastern ski resorts offer a wide variety of skiing experiences: Hunter Mountain (opposite, above) and Belleayre (bottom) in New York, both less than three hours from New York City, attract the urban skier. New Hampshire's Cannon Mountain (opposite, below), with 2,150 vertical feet, draws skiers in search of the big-mountain experience; Sugarloaf Mountain, Maine (below), appeals to the hearty and the heavyweights.

Colorado is ski country, and these mountains will leave the skier convinced. Snowmass (below), outside Aspen, is a four-mountain playground as popular with never-evers as it is with double-black-diamond skiers. Telluride (bottom), in the Southwest, is the Old West at its best. Crested Butte (opposite, above), thirty miles from Gunnison, attracts the no-glitz skier in search of skiing the way it used to be. Copper Mountain (opposite, below), seventy-five miles from Denver, is a front-range favorite with its own Club Med.

Not for the timid or faint of heart, the mountains pictured on these two pages will test any skier worth his NASTAR pin. Counterclockwise from left: Alta, Utah; Taos, New Mexico; Sun Valley, Idaho; and Jackson Hole, Wyoming

Skiers in the far West, three hours behind the East, are lucky—they always get the last run. These two pages: Spinning a web of fresh tracks on the snowfields of Oregon's Mount Hood. Opposite, inset: A bark eater struts styl- ishly through the timber at Alpine Meadows, California. Below, inset: The Cornice at California's Mammoth Mountain looks like fun skiing, until you get to the edge.

Utah skiing is as good as it gets. And most of it is within an hour's drive of Salt Lake City. Two favorites with skiers either close by or distant are Snowbird (below) and Park City (bottom).

PHOTOGRAPH CREDITS

Numbers refer to page numbers.